HIP
HOTELS

ESCAPE

HERBERT YPMA

HIP
HOTELS

ESCAPE

with 527 illustrations, 426 in color

Thames & Hudson

introduction

We live in an urban culture. The pressures and priorities of city life define the daily experience of most of us. But existing only to achieve goals and satisfy material needs is not enough. There has to be room in life for mystery, reflection and adventure. We crave the occasional return to essentials, if only to remind ourselves what the essentials really are.

Escape, getting away from it all, is the necessary flip-side of modern existence. Yet in a consumer-fuelled society, even this is not an easy task. There's too little time and too much choice – none of us wants to waste the few days or weeks we have on an experience that fails to live up to expectations. And of course we all have our own idea of what constitutes the perfect escape. Heaven, for some, is getting up before dawn to chase exotic wildlife with a camera in the African bush. Others are blissfully content chasing nothing more strenuous than a spaghetti *alla marinara* on the Mediterranean coast. *Hip Hotels Escape* offers plenty of options for both (and for those whose tastes fall somewhere in between) because the best escape venues *do* have a lot in common. None caters to large crowds – for the idea of escaping *en masse* is simply contradictory –

and none compromises in any way its incomparable location. In fact they do the opposite. All the best escape destinations amplify the attractions of their setting. Whether it be the rugged beauty of Wyoming, the gleaming expanse of Sweden's Arctic, the cowboy charm of the Camargue, the pristine immensity of the Australian outback, the idyll of a deserted island or the sophisticated sensuality of the Amalfi coast, all are made even more seductive by the hotel in their midst. This is what sets Hip Escape Hotels apart. All are in amazing locations that have become even more so through inspired design, sympathetic architecture and tireless attention to detail.

The power of architecture to define our experience is often underrated or misunderstood. A solitary lighthouse standing on Cape Horn serves to reinforce and emphasize the splendid isolation, just as a hotel built entirely in snow and ice focuses the magnificence of the Arctic. This is not architecture as academic debate or an obsession with technological novelty; simply the recognition of man's ability to enhance the beauty of a beautiful place.

el questro

Australia is a land of severe, almost bizarre contrasts. While ninety per cent of the population live in large metropolitan cities, more than ninety per cent of the land remains empty. The outback is incomprehensibly vast, a huge expanse of near-desert that registers on satellite photos as an enormous red splotch.

Surprisingly, although it dominates the country geographically and is never more than a few hours' drive away (whichever city you're in), the outback is as foreign to most Aussies as it is to visitors. Asia, Europe and America are the preferred destinations when Australians travel; not Uluru (Ayers Rock), Kakadu or the Bungle Bungles. The average Aussie has little knowledge of or spiritual contact with the outback. This is less surprising when you consider their lifestyle. They shop in malls, they drive Fords, BMWs and Toyotas, and they watch the same mindless television we all never admit to watching. Philip Adams, an Australian author, newspaper columnist and former advertising guru, once called Australia 'the most suburban nation in the world'.

Yet ironically it is the outback – the final frontier – that most visitors to Australia want to see. Its expanse is impossible to frame in words. To Australian author Peter Carey it is not a frontier but an unbounded space – as close as we can hope to come to infinity. It was this sense of vastness, unmatched on the planet, that made such an impression on Will Burrell, a young Etonian who came to Australia to do a stint as a jackaroo (cowboy) and ended up owning a million-acre cattle station in the far empty northwest of this continent.

Burrell's land is not the flat dust bowl swarming with flies that features in Castlemaine XXXX beer commercials. El Questro is in the Kimberley region of Western Australia, an area that boasts some of the world's most ancient and untouched geology. Craggy sandstone peaks rise above broad jagged gorges filled with crocodile-infested waters, while the flat land is studded with gum trees and pockets of tropical rainforest growing in microclimates created by the humid spray of waterfalls. In the months of December, January and February it is too wet to visit; a seasonal monsoon of monumental proportions turns everything from reddish dirt to terracotta sludge. (If you are thrown by the idea of a monsoon in the outback, remember that this continent is so vast that El Questro is actually closer to Jakarta than to Sydney).

At first, Burrell and his Australian wife Celia were planning to keep this piece of wilderness to themselves. The house that now hovers so spectacularly over the Chamberlain Gorge was designed by Queensland architect Geoffrey Pie to be their home. But along the way their plans evolved into the unique nature retreat that is El Questro. The name, by the way, means nothing – in any language. It's a word made up by the previous owners.

As a guest you are encouraged to experience to the full the extraordinary beauty of the property. Days start early, with coffee at 6 a.m. and then some exploring in the cool of the early morning. Excursions are rated from one to five according to difficulty by the rangers. From a broad list of choices, you might choose to climb Emma Gorge (a three) or hike out to the naturally heated Zebedee Springs (a one). Everyone returns to the homestead for breakfast at around 10.30, and the adventures resume later in the afternoon when the fierce Aussie sun has abated somewhat. El Questro is equipped with all the toys. There's a four-seater helicopter on

standby, specially designed four-wheel-drive jeeps, a stable of horses, and a flat-bottomed boat with electric engine for skimming along the gorge in perfect silence. In this isolated neck of the woods a helicopter is not a flash indulgence but a real necessity. Choppers are used throughout the outback to round up cattle – it's the only way.

Unlike most exclusive retreats, El Questro accommodates a range of budgets. First there are the basic (but air-conditioned) bungalows built along the Pentecost River. Then there is a collection of well-appointed tents pitched in Emma Gorge (though these are more *Out of Africa* than the sort of thing you would find in a mountaineering shop), and finally the original homestead itself. Whichever you choose – and some people opt for all three in turn – they all offer an experience of something genuinely magnificent: an Australia that remains exactly as it was millions of years before the first white man ever set foot on this enormous island.

address El Questro, PO Box 909, Kununurra, Western Australia 6743, Australia

telephone (61) 8 9169 1777   **fax** (61) 8 9169 1383

room rates from A$103

compass point

There are two kinds of Caribbean island. One plays host to huge cruise ships and their clientele, who sport dodgy colours like baby blue and buttermilk yellow, travel in packs and display an excessive fondness for duty-free shopping. The other is the white sand, blue sky, green water dream retreat that trades on its *lack* of duty-free shops, themed swimming pools, casinos or package tours and prides itself on its diminutive size and low-key approach.

New Providence island is both. On its northeast coast is Nassau, capital of the Bahamas, an archipelago just off the Florida peninsula comprising some seven hundred islets. Nassau is on the itinerary of many a cruise ship and is chock-a-block with duty-free jewellers, watch shops and liquor stores. Its streets are crammed with Hawaiian shirts, seersucker Bermuda shorts and shopping bags, and its colonial architecture is being choked to the point of extinction. Compass Point, on the other hand, at the far end of the island, is the polar opposite. It consists of a collection of timber cabins arranged along an idyllic point with not a shopping complex or nightclub in sight – nor even any other hotel. Nothing could be more different from downtown Nassau and its cruise-ship culture. Every cabin opens out to an unimpeded view of crystal-clear turquoise waters and a private beach is no more than a few hundred yards from any of the cabins.

But if this is a quiet place in terms of noise and neighbours it is anything but quiet in appearance. In fact it may well be the most colourful little retreat in the world. The Caribbean sense of colour is the heritage of the Afro-Latin roots of the region – not to mention a cheap and easy way to brighten up a basic wooden shack. Drawing on this historical fondness for bright colour, Hip Hotel entrepreneur Chris Blackwell (founder of Island Records) pulled out all the stops when it came to decorating the cabins of Compass Point. The result is a strikingly bold and funky statement of individuality that has obviously struck a chord here, and not just with the guests. Compass Point has become a bit of a hot spot with locals and with travellers staying in hotels nearby. The restaurant, perched on the very edge of the sea wall and looking out towards the lagoon that defines the resort, is booked solid every night. Decor, ambience and location have a lot to do with it, but so too does the food, which is exactly what one expects in the Caribbean: lots of seafood and lots of spices.

Spices were what first encouraged Columbus to sail west in the hope of finding a more direct route to the Far East. Instead he landed on the Bahamian island of Guanahani, renamed San Salvador by the Spanish. They soon enslaved the Taoi, the indigenous population, and transported them *en masse* to work mines and plantations elsewhere in the Caribbean. But the Bahamas had no gold, and their importance was soon eclipsed by other islands that did. Entirely depopulated, they eventually passed to the British in 1629. By that time, Spanish power in the region had long since waned and piracy was big business. Nassau was known as the Shanghai of the Caribbean. It was awash with shady characters, dirty money and vice. This era too came to a close through a clean-up campaign led by an ambitious governor general, who instigated grandiose agricultural projects and imported boatload after boatload of African slaves to work land concessions granted by the British crown.

Even so, the plantations of the Bahamas were no match for those of the American South. The first real boomtime for the Bahamas came during the American Civil War, when the southern states, faced with a total coastal trade blockade, instead used Nassau as a conduit for shipping their cotton to the mills of Lancaster, England. It was in this period that the first Grand Hotel was built to accommodate cotton merchants.

That marked the beginning of the tourism industry, now the primary wealth-producer for the Bahamian economy. Since the early part of the twentieth century the islands' ideal winter climate and pristine beaches have drawn tourists eager to escape the American winter. And with the invention of air-conditioning after World War II, the Bahamas developed into a year-round holiday destination. But don't assume popularity is always destructive. As even natives of other islands will confirm, the Bahamas still have the greenest water and the whitest beaches in the Caribbean.

address Compass Point, PO Box CB-13842, West Bay Street, Gambier, Nassau, The Bahamas
telephone (1) 242 327 4500 **fax** (1) 242 327 2398
room rates from US$215

amandari

Architecturally speaking, Amandari is the purest experience Bali has to offer.

Unlike all the other islands of the Indonesian archipelago, Bali has stayed true to its Hindu origins. Once upon a time all of Indonesia – Sumatra, Java, Borneo, Sulawesi and all the other three thousand-odd islands – were Hindu, a religion and culture brought over (along with Buddhism) from southern India via the age-old trade routes across the Indian Ocean.

Indonesians had an insatiable appetite for the crafts of India, and some of the most distinctive of indigenous craft traditions, including batik, derive ultimately from those of the neighbouring subcontinent. The first Dutch to trade in Southeast Asia exchanged ikat textiles purchased in southern India in return for Indonesian spices – an extraordinary bargain as far as the Europeans were concerned. The Hindu faith was adopted and adapted with the same vigour as were Indian crafts, and over the centuries Siva, Krishna, Vishnu and the rest of the Hindu pantheon acquired a definite Indonesian signature.

Today most of Indonesia is firmly Islamic and has been for several centuries. The majority of Hindu temples, statues and shrines have been destroyed. Bali remains the exception. Local tradition has it that as Islam swept through the island of Java in the fourteenth century AD, many of the nobility of the great kingdom of Majapahit fled to Bali in order to retain their Hindu beliefs. But in more recent centuries, had it not been for constant vigilance, Bali too might have lost its Hindu heritage. During Dutch colonial rule Muslim clerics were strictly forbidden to travel to Bali in order to prevent any weakening of its Hindu culture.

Without the gentle sophistication of Bali's predominant faith the island would not be the paradise it is today. In the people's mild disposition, their lifestyle, the way they dress, their relationship with their ancestors and their architecture and design, Bali is unique, and it is the island's Hindu heritage that makes it so. Age-old ritual cycles performed in the numerous temples continue to structure the lives of ordinary Balinese. A rich artistic and cultural tradition has survived here, its vigour unmatched elsewhere in Indonesia. Ceremonies from house blessings and weddings to colourful cremations are a way of life.

Sadly, however, the Balinese architectural tradition is in constant danger of dying out.

The Balinese sculptures are not just for decoration. They are shrines, and are adorned with flowers and incense daily

Amandari's buildings are arranged in the manner of a Balinese village

The traditional low-hanging roofs of the long rectangular halls are relieved by small open courtyards

All the rooms at Amandari feature a
bath in a separate outdoor pavilion

Amandari's authenticity is created by
traditional landscaping and architecture
true to the Balinese vernacular

Yellow banners signify a honeymoon
couple in residence

To a degree this is understandable. Bali is no economic backwater – far from it. It is part of a modern state with an expanding economy, and reinforced concrete construction is infinitely more practical than *alang alang* grass, coconut timber and lashed bamboo when it comes to putting up shops, warehouses and other utilitarian buildings.

That is why Amandari in Kedewatan village is so special. It recreates faithfully the original architecture of Bali, which derives ultimately from that of southern India. Architect Peter Muller not only reintroduced traditional forms and materials, but he also stayed faithful to the layout of a Balinese village. The authenticity is what makes it so captivating.

Guests don't get a room, they get a house, each one positioned along narrow stone-paved walkways that echo the arrangement of a traditional Balinese village. Decorative stonework adorns the entrance to each guest villa and, in a time-honoured practice, vertical yellow banners are set outside those occupied by honeymoon couples. Built in teak and volcanic stone, they are surrounded by courtyards that create complete privacy. Each house is a lofty structure with a ceiling that reaches a height of thirty feet in the centre and tapers tent-like towards the four corners. Roofs are thatched in traditional *alang alang* grass supported by a lattice of lashed bamboo that rests on timber columns cut from coconut trees. In every detail of materials and design this is an architecture perfectly suited to the tropical climate – the high ceilings provide plenty of circulation while the low overhangs keep the sun out.

Perched high above the Ayung River in central Bali, Amandari offers tranquil views of the island's lush countryside, terraced rice paddies and active volcanoes. In the far distance you can even make out the Indian Ocean, some twenty-five miles away. In Sanskrit Amandari means 'the place of peaceful spirits'. It's certainly the perfect introduction to the peace and hospitality of traditional Bali.

address Amandari, Ubud, Bali, Indonesia
telephone (62) 361 975 333 **fax** (62) 361 975 335
room rates from US$525

amankila

For years Bali was not on my travel itinerary. It had a reputation as the Costa Brava of Asia, an inexpensive fun-in-the-sun destination for Australian package tourists. Kuta Beach in particular was said to be a complete circus, nothing but raucous drunks and Bo Derek-style beaded plaits. And it is. But thankfully all the fast food, cheap bars and giant water-slides are concentrated in one small corner of the island. Beyond Kuta Beach is the real Bali – the Bali of small villages, rice paddies, Hindu temples and lush jungle. Bali remains sparsely populated, and as a result there are still plenty of villages without billboards and beaches unspoilt by tacky fake-Tahitian resort architecture.

Candi Dasa on the north-east coast of the island fits the bill perfectly. It was here that Adrian Zecha, impresario of the Aman phenomenon, chose to build one of the most spectacular examples of resort architecture anywhere in the world. Amankila is perched on a cliff face overlooking the Lombok Strait, hundreds of metres above an isolated beach. Its structures were built on a series of plateaus carved into the side of an impossibly steep hill. With everything on different levels, Amankila becomes a carefully orchestrated series of

vistas, the most dramatic formed by the three successive 'spill pools' that cascade down the vertical face of the cliff. Despite being among the most photographed pools on earth, the real thing still does impress.

Of course spectacular cascades of water are nothing new in the history books. All the most beautiful gardens of Renaissance Italy had them, and for exactly the same reason: to knock people's socks off. These are pools so beautiful that you don't have to get wet to enjoy them. In fact I noticed quite a few guests who did not swim, but who were nonetheless impossible to pry away from the poolside. Like all of Amankila the pools are a sheer visual indulgence. From the restaurants to the bar to the beach club to the shaded privacy of the individual thatched *bales* surrounding pool and beach, every detail, every element of form, texture and finish has been painstakingly thought through by Aman architect Ed Tuttle.

Virtually nothing about Amankila resembles a conventional hotel. First of all there are no rooms. Each guest or couple have their own private bungalow on their own level, which is connected to all the other levels and facilities via an elaborate series of stone stairs that snake their way throughout the property.

From every house there is a panoramic view over emerald green waters that can be enjoyed from the outdoor living room on the terrace or inside from the enormous canopy bed.

Even so, it's hard to pinpoint exactly what makes the Amankila experience so seductive. Perhaps it's the feeling that you have the whole place to yourself, or because the bath oils and shampoo are presented in beautiful glass bottles, or because the closets are big enough for Elton John's wardrobe. And the service, of course, is legendary, true to Aman form – frankly, the Amankila's attention to detail makes even the Ritz look shabby.

Then there are the facilities. A maximum of seventy guests get to share four pools (three cascading spectacles and a serious forty-five-metre lap pool by the beach club), three restaurants (two with a view and one by the beach club pool), a bar, a library, and a beach shack stocked with every conceivable toy for venturing onto the water, from a catamaran to a windsurfer.

The commitment to quality continues with the food. The chef at Amankila used to work at Level 41, one of the finest restaurants in Sydney (a worthwhile recommendation given Sydney's reputation for food). The menu is both Asian and continental, though its Indonesian offerings are the more interesting. Admittedly I was sceptical at first of Indonesian food displayed and arranged in a nouvelle cuisine style: a triangular mound of saffron rice and a few skewers of artfully arranged chicken saté seemed to be trying a little too hard to appeal to Western eyes. Yet the fact is that many visitors who frequent Bali on a regular basis will assure you that Amankila offers some of the best Indonesian food on Bali.

All told, Amankila is an impressive place. The sheer scale and spectacle of Ed Tuttle's design will astonish you. The food, facilities and lavish attention to detail will spoil you. But none of it would count for anything if it were not also for Amankila's merciful distance from the chaos of Kuta.

address Amankila, Manggis, Bali, Indonesia
telephone (62) 363 41333 **fax** (62) 363 41555
room rates from US$525

waka di ume

In certain circles – discriminating circles – Waka di Ume is considered the hottest place in Ubud. Set in the foothills of Bali's central mountain range, Ubud is the most spiritual and artistic destination on the island. Here Hindu traditions are intact, people still work the rice paddies and life goes on without taking too much note of tourism. Sure, there is the odd souvenir shop and a few tea rooms, but by and large the integrity and authenticity of centuries of Balinese Hindu culture remain intact.

Ubud attracts artists in part because it always has. Long before the first Western artists settled here in the thirties, Ubud was a centre for Balinese art. Different villages on the island have always specialized in particular crafts. Batubulan, for example, is renowned as a village of stone workers, Mas is a village of woodcarvers, Celuk is famed for its gold and silver jewelry, Peliatan for musical instruments, and Ubud for its artists. Perhaps this tradition is responsible for Ubud's laid-back atmosphere; or maybe the temperatures, which are far less extreme than on the coast, just make life that bit more comfortable. Whatever the reason, Ubud is an undeniably groovy place, and Waka di Ume captures the essence of the area better than any other hotel.

Owned, designed and managed by young Balinese architect Ketut Siandana and his two brothers, Waka di Ume is a stunning complex of cottages arranged on a long thin strip of land along the top of a rice field. It's described by Waka's management as 'the Bali you came for', and they are not far off. With a dormant volcano behind and the view dominated on all sides by a never-ending cascade of water-filled rice paddies, Waka di Ume fulfils our every fantasy of exotic and mystical Bali.

From the outset Waka was designed to be different. Its strength is that it succeeds in combining the traditions of Bali with a very contemporary sense of architectural modernity. So, for example, roofs are thatched in fragrant *alang alang* grass while the floors are of polished concrete tiles. Furniture includes the odd piece in stainless steel and bamboo, while bathrooms juxtapose polished native stone with vast expanses of glass that look over terraced rice fields. Waka feels very Balinese, but in a relaxed and uncontrived manner. Siandana understands the need for Bali to retain its special magic and yet at the same time to move forward. As a result his work succeeds in introducing traditional Balinese aesthetics to a modern style.

The design of Waka di Ume is modern in a distinctively Balinese way; the staff wear the traditional sarong

Waka di Ume has mosquito nets that really work – elaborate constructions that hang straight, not in your face

Located on the rim of a cascade of rice paddies, the restaurant has a view straight from a postcard

Waka di Ume is a family affair. The architect is the owner and his sister made the mosquito nets

Contemporary design is juxtaposed with traditional Balinese forms

A quirky Balinese still life decorates the start of a passageway that culminates in a descending series of pools

It is this design sense that pervades every part of the hotel. The two-storey restaurant at the entrance offers a more Western-style space downstairs, complete with tables and chairs, and an upstairs level more evocative of a 'long house', where guests sit on floor pillows and eat Balinese cuisine from low tables. At the other end of the long thin property is a large, elegant building with spectacular views over the rice fields. This was purpose-built as a massage centre. Inside it is sparse and open-plan, with a vast 'loft'-style space at the top specifically for meditation that overlooks a spectacular multi-tiered cascade pool built in stone. Positioned along this stretched-out space defined by the restaurant, massage centre and pools are the sixteen cabins and cottages that constitute the accommodation. Stone paths connecting individual houses are widely spaced for graphic effect, wind chimes hang from the outside corners of most buildings, and stone statues of Hindu gods punctuate the paths and courtyards of the property.

As is so often the case with Hip Hotels, Waka is very much a family affair. Ketut was the architect, his brother takes care of marketing, another brother is in charge of finance, and their sister makes all the incredibly intricate mosquito-net curtaining that screens the beautifully designed beds. It doesn't hurt, of course, that the family also owns the luxurious Oberoi resorts on Bali and Lombok. The Siandana brothers are second generation hoteliers, and with their dynamic new Waka group they are laying the foundations for a new, more environmentally and culturally aware tourism in Bali. So in addition to managing this hotel, operating four-wheel-drive adventures into Bali's highlands and maintaining a series of large catamarans for sailing expeditions, they also have a few other Waka hotels in the pipeline. And what do the brothers do when they have a moment to spare? They share a passion for old motorbikes. Three young Hindus on Harleys – that really captures what Waka is all about.

---

address Waka di Ume Resort, Jalan Sueta, Ubud, Bali, Indonesia

telephone (62) 361 973178   **fax** (62) 361 973179

room rates from US$115

blancaneaux lodge

Anyone who has ever seen *Heart of Darkness*, the fascinatingly revealing documentary story of Francis Ford Coppola's struggle against formidable odds to make *Apocalypse Now*, would be surprised, astounded even, that the acclaimed film director had ever willingly set foot in another jungle. Yet the dense equatorial green of the Philippine jungle obviously made a deep impression, for that's exactly how Blancaneaux Lodge got started – as a private retreat built by Coppola for himself and his family in the tropical rainforest of Belize.

Belize is an enigmatic and exotic little nation, and it fits that the maker of a film of such surreal complexity and dark humour as *Apocalypse Now* should have a retreat here. (I certainly can't imagine Coppola with a cottage in the Hamptons.) The only English-speaking country in Central America, Belize was a British colony until 1981, though its 200,000-strong population still consider the queen of England their monarch. It has the world's second largest coral reef and abundant rainforests hiding spectacular Mayan ruins.

It's an unlikely, almost absurd country that suits Coppola well – and vice versa. Ending up here wasn't even really by conscious choice. When, in 1982, he read of Belize's recently gained independence, he followed an impulse and flew down to propose what he saw as a unique opportunity for the new nation. He was convinced that with their own satellite, they could become a major hub of international telecommunications. But the Belize ministers didn't see it that way at all, and the famous filmmaker was left with time on his hands there and little else for his efforts. Like a script from one of his own movies, he followed a barman's tips about excursions into the rainforest and came across an abandoned lodge. Deciding this was a place he could write, he bought it. It's a good story.

A piece of jungle high up in the mountains beside a sparkling river with a waterfall – it really is as idyllic as it sounds. But the practicalities of paradise proved a major feat of organization. Each time the Coppola family wanted to head down to Belize, a military-style preparation had to be unleashed: arrange supplies, fire up the generator, check the road is clear … in the end it all became too much. The solution was to go to stage two: invest in infrastructure (more accommodation, better services, improved supplies) and convert Blancaneaux Lodge into a small, exclusive, eco-friendly retreat.

That's when Mexican architect Manuel Mestre entered the picture. Coppola had seen his sensitive, culturally appropriate work for other private clients and, Coppola being Coppola, this was not going to be a project compromised intellectually, pragmatically or, as it turns out, financially. The result was clever, creative and … expensive. By all accounts Coppola is an ideas-driven personality who is not only used to getting his way but to doing so against the odds. Disregarding all advice he even insisted on developing a hydroelectric power source for the property. The plant (which took 400,000 tons of sand to build) now churns out enough electricity for round-the-clock power, and then some. It still gives him a thrill, Coppola says, to sit at his laptop in his thatched villa and know that the power illuminating his screen is generated by the sparkling Privassion River below.

It must be safe to say that this is the only tropical mountain retreat equipped with a proper wood-fired pizza oven from Italy, not to mention an espresso machine complete with bean-roasting apparatus. And of course a decent pizza is not possible without fresh ingredients, so it was decided to grow vegetables on the premises. Deer took the first crop, but a sturdy new fence now ensures that the kitchen garden provides the produce used for the pizzas and all the other dishes.

But make no mistake, the real star here is the setting. The river water is clear enough to drink, the steamy climate is tempered by the altitude and for most of the year there are no mosquitoes. The spectacular Mayan ruins of Caracol are ninety minutes away. Blancaneaux is a place dense with beauty. The beneficiaries of Coppola's highly productive and fearless imagination are the guests. Quite simply, you get to enjoy all the fruits of his creativity and his high standards in wine, food and quality of life without expending any of the energy (not to mention money). Coppola tells a joke that goes: how do you make a small fortune in Belize? Answer? Bring down a large one.

address Blancaneaux Lodge, Central Farm, PO Box B, Cayo District, Belize

telephone (501) 92 3878   **fax** (501) 92 3919

room rates from US$115

hotel explora

'The joy of the remote' is Explora's motto. Its founding purpose is to allow you to experience territories previously accessible only to the most serious trekkers and climbers. Explora is in the virgin wilderness of Chile's Patagonia, a labyrinth of fjords, glaciers, icebergs, turquoise lakes and jagged peaks, in a land populated by nanus, penguins and llamas. The hotel perches spectacularly above a waterfall on the Rio Paine, in the 600-square-mile Torres del Paine National Park, so named because in the local Indian language *paine* is the word for glacier-blue. It lives up to its motto in very convincing fashion. To get here you fly from Santiago, Chile's cosmopolitan capital, to Punta Arenas on the Strait of Magellan, the southernmost city in the world. Short of Antarctica, Patagonia is about as far from civilization as you can get.

Its remoteness was the inspiration behind Bruce Chatwin's classic work *In Patagonia*. As he explains: 'The Cold War woke in me a passion for geography.... In the late forties the Cannibal of the Kremlin shadowed our lives … and yet we hoped to survive the blast. We started an emigration committee and made plans to settle in some far corner of the earth. The war would come in the northern hemisphere so we looked to the southern. We ruled out Australia and New Zealand and fixed on Patagonia as the safest place on earth … somewhere to live when the rest of the world blew up….'

Samarkand, Timbuktu, Patagonia … there are few locations so untouched by the rapid rise of global travel that they can still conjure dreams of legend and adventure. It's even rarer for these places to live up to one's dreams. This is one that does. Seeing the Hotel Explora for the first time, singular and isolated, looking for all the world like a tycoon's yacht run aground, you cannot help but wonder how it got here. Designed to withstand Patagonia's ferocious winds, Explora is the project of Pedro Ibanez, a Chilean multi-millionaire who believes passionately that urbanites should experience the wonders of nature – starting with his own backyard, Chile's 'outback'.

The first step towards building this modern and luxurious thirty-room lodge in pristine wilderness was to win a National Forest Service competition. The Chilean authorities are particularly protective of their extraordinary natural set piece. Ibanez not only won the competition, he also drew up a comprehensive manifesto for his new hospitality organization.

Explora's dramatic setting, as viewed through a bathroom window

Only llamas are equipped to deal with Patagonia's soaring, bleak, isolated peaks

Explora is perched beside the Rio Paine in the middle of six hundred square miles of national park

Created by Chilean entrepreneur Pedro Ibanez, Explora exists to encourage excursions into Chile's wilderness

The warmth and intimacy of the interior compensates for the 'outdoors in all weather' policy during the day

The architecture of Patagonia's Explora is one of extreme contrast – of pristine modernity versus untamed nature

Firmly opposed to mass tourism, Explora's approach is one that the American media has taken to calling 'eco-luxe'. It embraces not only a profound respect for the natural environment but also a supportive empathy for the local people and culture. In practice that means every detail is carefully planned to minimize the impact on the environment, from the size of excursion groups (no more than eight people) to the need for the architecture to complement the local landscape and culture.

All this may sound perfectly logical, even self-evident, but in a place as remote as Patagonia there are no second chances: one cannot simply go down the road to another establishment. From the moment your plane touches down in Punta Arenas you're in their hands. The hotel is therefore a crucial part of the equation. It's difficult to think of anything Hotel Explora might have left out. All thirty rooms have spectacular views, the enclosed lap pool situated alongside the running river is heated to tropical temperatures, food is flown in from Santiago, there are saunas for post-excursion recovery and intimate lounging spaces with cowhide-covered easy chairs beside large open fires – ideal for drinking their 'Pisco Sours' (hey, I climbed the Valle del Frances glacier – I deserved it!).

Every day, regardless of the weather, there are five different options from a wide range of excursions the hotel has developed, all rated according to difficulty. Undertaken in the company of highly experienced guides, they include climbing, trekking, glacier hiking, mountain biking, riding, kayaking and bird watching. Explora emphasizes that it is not a 'sport hotel' and does not want to drive guests into adrenalin-fuelled, competitive nature experiences. But on the other hand you will not be allowed to use the weather as an excuse to stay indoors. In the Explora philosophy, a snowstorm can be just as enjoyable as a sunny day. They are right – even if some of us need a gentle push before we will get out there and discover it for ourselves.

postal address   Gochile, Suecia 84, suite 82, Santiago, Chile

telephone (56) 2 251 2625   **fax** (56) 2 251 5882

room rates   from US$1347 (for a minimum three-night stay)

vatulele

Vatulele, a name meaning 'Ringing Rock' in Fijian, is the small Pacific island chosen by Henry Crawford and Martin Livingston to realize their vision of a contemporary retreat incorporating indigenous Polynesian traditions. Located just south of the main island of Fiji, Vatulele has only one village, whose residents fish and farm just enough for their own subsistence. They also make traditional *tapa* cloth from the bark of the mulberry tree. Life carries on pretty much as it did before the white man arrived. Crawford, an Australian Emmy-award-winning producer, and Livingston, a fifth-generation European Fijian, were determined to keep it that way.

The resort's eighteen huts or *bures* were built on land leased from a group of native landowners, and were designed to make a minimal impact on the island's pristine topography. All the materials – sand, timber, structured poles, cement – were imported from the mainland, carefully unloaded and positioned by hand. No construction crane touched the shores of Ringing Rock. Clearing the site took one hundred men three months, using nothing more than knives. Particular care was taken to ensure that the palm trees fringing the island's perfect lagoon were not touched.

Today the palms shade the guest *bures* that stand between them. Vatulele is a true 'toes in the sand island', as one visiting journalist described it, devoid of all references to Western lifestyles – there are no telephones, fax machines, cars, paved roads, electricity wires, noise or commotion. This same loose and sensuous approach is expressed in the design and architecture of the resort. Crawford and Livingston planned to combine all the best ingredients of Pacific culture into a single expression. To do so they turned – improbably, you might think – to an American architect, Doug Nelson. Based in Santa Fe, Nelson is known for work that brilliantly incorporates the indigenous style of New Mexico into contemporary architecture and design. Given the many similarities between Polynesian and Native North American cultures, he was not such an unlikely choice after all.

The most striking cultural signatures on Vatulele are the traditional Fijian roof structures. These allow rising heat to disperse through the loose thatch, keeping the *bures* cool without the need for artificial air-conditioning. But they go far beyond mere functionality. Their artistry is an exquisite example of the possibilities of Pacific craft.

Bound together by woven rope stained in the traditional and distinctively Polynesian shades of pink and green, they are inspiring pieces of handiwork that copy the original island methods of roof construction. The *bures* and their magnificent ceilings are a powerful component of Pacific style.

But the ceilings are just the beginning. Throughout the retreat, by imaginative ways and means, Crawford, Livingston and their architect have incorporated genuine elements of Polynesian culture. The main *bure* is decorated with traditional weapons, while *tapa* cloth made by the local villagers hangs on the walls of each individual guest villa. A motif extracted from a typical *tapa* pattern is used as a recurring logo in the floor tiles and other architectural detailing.

Yet despite the restraint of its concept and design, Vatulele is not at all about 'roughing it'. This South Pacific hideaway knows how to cater to people accustomed to luxury. Each *bure* is more house than hut, furnished with separate living and sleeping areas and equipped with an expansive bathroom. And because of the initial effort to preserve the palm trees along the lagoon front, each *bure* is hidden from the next by a veil of South Pacific green. Everything here, from the architecture to the food (which includes delicious gourmet pizzas from a wood-fired oven), is both exceptional and in total harmony with the surroundings. Guests are invited to explore the forests, waterfalls, cliffs and caves of the island, while those who choose to spend time in their *bures* are surrounded by authentic Fijian tradition.

Commitment to authenticity has admittedly come at a price. Twice to date, hurricanes have flattened the lovely roofs of the *bures*, and each time they have been replaced with the same intricate, labour-intensive structures. As a Pacific development project, Vatulele is a trailblazer. It has set the standard by which all tourist projects have come to be judged. Ecologically responsible, culturally sensitive, geographically appropriate – and simple.

postal address Vatulele, Worldwide Reservation Office, 1 Greville Street, Clovelly, Sydney, NSW 2031, Australia

telephone (61) 2 9665 8700 **fax** (61) 2 9665 7833

room rates from US$1078

la bastide de moustiers

Situated in the spectacular Gorges du Verdon – possibly one of the most photographed locations in all of France – the charm of La Bastide de Moustiers is magnified by the rugged beauty of the surroundings. Full of canyons, gullies, lakes, cliffs and caves, this is the favourite area in France for summer outdoor sports. While other regions of France are known for their marshes (the Camargue), their wineries (Bouche du Rhône) or their colourful fields (Vars), Haute Provence is famed for its craggy granite faces and impressive gorges. No more than an hour and a half from Aix-en-Provence by car, this part of the south of France still looks and feels like a wilderness.

The location was a perfect backdrop for Alain Ducasse's venture. Most famous for his three-Michelin-star Monte Carlo restaurant Louis XV, he has always maintained that the ingredient should be given top billing. But the message has perhaps in the past been diluted by the grandeur of his Monaco restaurant. So on acquiring an old run-down *bastide* or stone farmhouse in Haute Provence, Ducasse created an establishment that demonstrates his obsession with fresh produce. Unlike some hotels famous for their cuisine, there is nothing grand about La Bastide de Moustiers. The

name of the game for guests is to experience the transformation of freshly picked fruits and vegetables into incredible dishes. The main kitchen, the pastry kitchen and the kitchen garden take centre stage. Crates of tomatoes, aubergines, courgettes, melons, figs and green beans are scattered around the hallways, stacked on the staircase and haphazardly arranged all around the main entrance. The point of it all is that the food and its preparation *is* the experience.

Staying at La Bastide de Moustiers conjures up all of the most sensuous and seductive passages of Peter Mayle's *A Year in Provence*. The wild beauty of the landscape, the charm of slightly dilapidated stone farmhouses and the authenticity of age-old sleepy villages are the backdrop to Mayle's prose and Ducasse's cuisine alike. The accommodation, appropriately, has not ventured too far from rural tradition. Interiors are light, colourful and very French, and the rooms are much like the table settings: pleasant, stylish but not overpowering. Pretty floral fabrics, whitewashed cupboards, terracotta-tiled floors, linen blinds and the odd Provençal antique reinforce an overall atmosphere of relaxed authenticity.

Set against the imposing rock faces
of Haute Provence, the location could
not be more scenic

In summer the dining room tables
are kept bare except for the odd,
strategically placed piece of fresh fruit

Typically French and typically
Provençal, the rooms combine rustic
simplicity with the odd grand touch

'The ingredient is queen' is the motto
of superchef Alain Ducasse

An old wrought-iron gate leads from
the main terrace into the landscaped
grounds

A tart of freshly peeled tomatoes on
a bed of mint is a favourite dish

Despite the rural authenticity of the
Provençal farmhouse, bathrooms are
untypically spacious and luxurious

The gilded detail of a Louis XV chair
is a reminder of Ducasse's famous
Louis XV restaurant in Monte Carlo

Field flowers growing wild are another
reminder of La Bastide's rural setting

La Bastide de Moustiers: literally, the farmhouse of the village of Moustiers

A fresh fig tart, a Provençal speciality, made in the Bastide's own pastry kitchen

The dining room is a cosy space used only in the winter

Crates of fresh produce are always to be found around the property

Each guest room is named after a local flower or herb

Whenever possible, through most of the year, meals are served outdoors on the terrace

White and pristine and drenched with intense Provençal light, the bathrooms are as fresh and light as the food

All fruits and vegetables are delivered daily or picked straight from the kitchen garden

The colours of Provence, which Van Gogh so successfully captured, are also the colours of La Bastide de Moustiers

The highlight may be the food, but there is certainly no shortage of things to do between eating: mountaineering, riding, hang-gliding mountain-biking and kayaking are just some of the sports for which this part of France is well known. For the less adventurous, it's enough to walk to the village, wander through the markets, stop for a coffee and play some *boules*. The village of Moustiers-Ste-Marie, perhaps because of its precarious and dramatic setting, has escaped the onslaught of 'boutiques and banks', the architectural hangover of tourism. Within the grounds of La Bastide de Moustiers, Ducasse has managed to cater to contemporary demands with typical style. There is a pool, but it is very cleverly hidden into the landscape, so that although it has an extraordinary view of the surrounding valley, it is not visible from the approach to the farm and does not disturb the natural beauty of the setting.

The fun of La Bastide de Moustiers is that it is a real experience in which you feel you are learning something about traditional Provence:

its prevailing architecture (stone farmhouses), its landscape and its cuisine. As at all places renowned for their food, there is no menu. The chef decides the dishes of the day, and at La Bastide this is done with great creativity and originality. Traditional French dishes are twisted, contorted and reinvented using unexpected ingredients and unusual combinations. A typical invention is a *millefeuille* of crispy bacon strips interspersed with pumpkin purée. A meal at La Bastide de Moustiers consists of a succession of dishes, most of which you won't have encountered before – and that is the major attraction. Since the hotel opened in spring 1995, it has made a huge impact on the international scene. Leading fashion, travel and design magazines have been standing in line to splash its food and atmosphere across their pages. So ironically, despite Ducasse's best efforts to keep it simple, there is little he can do to stop the odd helicopter filled with Côte d'Azure jet-setters dropping in for lunch.

address La Bastide de Moustiers, Chemin de Quinson, 04360 Moustiers-Ste-Marie, France

telephone (33) 492 70 47 47 **fax** (33) 492 70 47 48

room rates from FF 850

la mirande

In its review of La Mirande, *Le Figaro* predicted that this Avignon town house would become 'a place of pilgrimage for men and women of taste'. It's easy to see why. Anyone who has known even the vaguest twitch of Francophilia could not help but be impressed by the splendid heritage this hotel evokes. You would be hard-pressed to find a more beautiful or comprehensive embodiment of France's unparalleled contribution to several centuries of the decorative arts.

La Mirande is housed in a distinguished city mansion located directly opposite the Palais du Papes, the seat of five successive popes in the fourteenth century, when the Roman Catholic Church was ruled from Avignon. The house dates from the fifteenth century. It was built around the charred foundations of a cardinal's palace that was destroyed by fire in 1411. Inside, the contributions of all of France's different decorative periods blend together in one exuberant and perfectly aristocratic mix. A Renaissance dining room with coffered ceilings, a Louis XV Rococo library with chinoiserie painted panels, an eighteenth-century private dining room, a salon in the Belle Epoque–Rothschild style, a winter breakfast room with all the neoclassical restraint of Louis XVI, plus an impressively detailed baroque facade: La Mirande has the layered opulence that testifies to centuries of wealth and cultivated taste. It is a seamless mix of all the different styles and epochs of French decorative history – almost a catalogue of French historical style.

So you would be forgiven for supposing that all this were the product of age, good breeding and inheritance. The surprising truth is that it was created virtually from scratch. It's true that this magnificent house had been in the Pamard family, one of Avignon's oldest and most prestigious clans, for more than two hundred years, but their contribution to the city, alas, did not include an exquisite interior. Far from it. What Achim and Hannelore Stein found when they bought the house in 1987 was a sinister nineteenth-century gothic interior that had the dubious reputation of being 'the darkest house in Avignon'. Both passionate about art and antiques, the new owners set themselves the challenge of creating an interior with all the prestige and integrity that the house might have had if circumstances had been different. For most this would have been a stretch of visual imagination too far.

For Achim Stein, a retired civil engineer whose final project had been to mastermind the construction of Jedda airport in Saudi Arabia, it was exactly the kind of challenge that he and his wife were looking for.

Working with the renowned Parisian decorator François-Joseph Graf, the Steins devised a decorative scheme for the property on the basis of a hypothetical premise, namely that Pierre Mignard – son of the famous court painter Nicolas Mignard and designer of the house's baroque facade in the late seventeenth century – had gone on to design the interior. Then an allowance was made for all the improvements and alterations to the original scheme that would have been made by a wealthy family over several generations as fashions rose and fell. According to Martin Stein, the son and present creative director of the whole La Mirande enterprise (which also includes a cookery school), the clearly defined aim was to create the impression that it had always been like this.

The end result is utterly convincing: the interior looks and feels like the well-preserved heritage of three hundred years of refined living. In reality it took not three centuries but just two years, about eleven million dollars, and an extraordinary attention to detail to achieve. No effort or expense was spared: curtains throughout the hotel are lined with silk; windowpanes are hand-blown glass; handblocked wallpapers were crumpled before hanging to create texture and patina; and the banister was copied from the stone entrance to nearby Château de Barbentane. The rooms are all different and are furnished with antiques gathered from France and overseas. Renaissance ceilings were restored, and wherever possible reclaimed stone, timber and tiles were used in preference to anything new.

The outcome of all this meticulous effort is the perfect escape – a spectacular journey through the most splendid chapters in the history of the French decorative arts, amid the charm and refinement of historical Avignon.

address La Mirande, 4 place de la Mirande, F-84000 Avignon, France
telephone (33) 4 90 85 93 93   **fax** (39) 4 90 86 26 85
room rates from FF 1700

le mas de peint

If there's a French equivalent of 'Marlboro Country', then this is it. Le Mas de Peint is a converted ranch in the Camargue, a sun-bleached marshland south of Arles home to black bulls, white horses and colourful gypsies. The music here is flamenco (the 'Gypsy Kings' are from the Camargue), the favourite spectator sport is a local version of bullfighting in which agile *razeteurs* try to pluck a coloured ribbon from the bull's horns and exit the ring before being skewered, and men and women proudly wear the brightly coloured block-printed fabrics made famous by companies like Souleiado. The Camargue is quite unlike any other part of France. There are no chateaux – only simple whitewashed ranches; and there is no legacy of aristocracy – ranch owners and their 'cowboys' work side by side. In style it has more in common with New Mexico, or the *estancias* of Argentina than with the manicured refinement of northern France.

Jacques Bon, proprietor of Le Mas de Peint, was born and raised in the Camargue, and he takes his cowboy heritage very seriously. He still takes part in the round-up of horses and cattle, often spending the better part of the day on a horse (a white one, of course), and wears only the uniform of the Camargue cowboy –

paisley-printed shirts, moleskins and riding boots. Together with his wife Lucille, an architect, he decided a decade ago to convert part of his family ranch into a small luxury hotel. But he is not out of the ranching business altogether. He still keeps forty white horses and three hundred black bulls.

From the very beginning both Jacques and Lucille Bon had very clear ideas about what kind of place it should be. Above all they believed it should retain the rugged character that is so much the signature of the Camargue. They did not want their guests to be cosseted and pampered in a five-star, 'yes sir, no sir' kind of way. That is not the way of the Camargue. The atmosphere they had in mind was that of friends coming over to help round up the horses. They would naturally eat in the kitchen, spend the day on horseback and collapse at night in a neat but not too 'tarted up' room. No glitz, no glamour, just the rosy glow of genuine hospitality, good food and being outdoors all day. The experience of Le Mas de Peint comes remarkably close to this vision. Everybody eats together in the kitchen, rooms are spacious but sparsely furnished, and guests are encouraged to ride along to help round up the herds.

The famous white horses of the Camargue are born grey; they turn white as they get older

Le Mas de Peint's pared-down decor shows an architect's preference for neutral tones and natural fabrics

The wild rice displayed on a table in the reception area is a special hybrid variety grown on the property

Le Mas de Peint is a typical *mas* or stone farmhouse converted into a small luxurious hotel

Embroidered white linen and old brass beds: this is farmhouse style with a minimalist twist

The Camargue is France's cowboy country. The hotel interior reflects the region's ranch culture

Every evening around ten there is a ritual that the Bons adhere to faithfully. Jacques and his wife emerge from their private quarters and do the rounds in the kitchen, greeting and chatting with their guests. On the first night that I witnessed this ritual Jacques Bon appeared like a French rodeo star. He was wearing moleskins with a red pinstripe down the side and a red silk paisley-patterned shirt. He speaks not a word of English, but that didn't deter him from slapping backs, cracking jokes and working the room like a politician. The next day it was the same – only this time he wore black moleskins and a black silk paisley shirt. With his handlebar moustache and his colourful 'cowboy threads', seventy-six-year-old Jacques Bon is quite a character. Magazine reviews have dubbed him the Jack Palance of the Camargue. He and Lucille are the perfect hosts for a genuine Camargue experience. He adds the colourful local flavour and she contributes the urbane design touch that makes Le Mas de Peint such a pleasurable retreat.

For despite Jacques Bon's insistence that he doesn't want to pamper guests, Le Mas de Peint is significantly more luxurious than your average Camargue ranch. The guest rooms are large, bed linen is immaculate (and embroidered with the brand of the ranch) and the *en suite* bathrooms are of a size and design standard you would expect in a sophisticated city hotel. A large swimming pool with a stone-tiled terrace is hidden in one of the paddocks and one of the large barns has been converted for use as a party space.

I had always rather cynically assumed that the famous white horses, black bulls, gypsies and whitewashed ranches of the Camargue were about as real as windmills and wooden shoes in Holland – in other words just something staged for the tourists. But unlike other parts of Europe the Camargue has not been sanitized by tourism and a uniform suburban culture. Here, people cling fiercely to their way of life. Where else could you meet a character like Jacques Bon?

address Hôtel Le Mas de Peint, Le Sambuc, 13200 Arles, France
telephone (33) 4 90 97 20 62   **fax** (33) 4 90 97 22 20
room rates from FF 1195

les fermes de marie

In the heart of the sophisticated Haute Savoie village of Megève, Fermes de Marie is everything you could expect of a place in the Alps. With rugged weather-worn timber beams, old terracotta-tiled floors, panelled walls, rustic pottery, red gingham, naive paintings, simple wooden chairs and roaring fires, this hotel embodies every romantic vision you can muster of the perfect chalet in the snow.

Fermes de Marie is exemplary of the traditional style of the Haute Savoie. This is the French equivalent of the Tirol (minus the yodelling and *lederhosen*) where, as in Austria, the houses have a gingerbread look, with peaked roofs, small windows and carved wooden balustrades, the people are hearty and gregarious, and the food is rich and heavy. It's almost impossible not to be charmed by *le style Savoyard*, with its emphasis on texture, warmth, comfort and bright colours – especially when it's the real thing.

Jean-Louis and Jocelyne Sibuet, who opened Les Fermes de Marie in 1989, grew up in these mountains. They are real Savoyards and their creation is to a large degree an extension of their own lifestyle. That's not to say, however, that Les Fermes de Marie was easy to create. Today it's a hotel complete with indoor swimming pool, three different restaurants, a fitness centre and beauty spa, a games room, a parking garage for fifty cars, and more. Only a decade ago it was just an idea and a ragtag assembly of abandoned cow sheds, hay lofts and mountain refuges that the Sibuets had systematically collected in and around the Haute Savoie. The idea was to give these bundles of old, weathered timber a new life as the architectural core of an authentic Savoyard hotel experience.

There was some irony in the Sibuets' choice of Megève, the most chichi of all French ski resorts, to build their farm complex. The farmers who sold them their dilapidated sheds, *bergeries* and barns would be dumbstruck to find them occupying prime real estate in the centre of one of the most aristocratic villages in France. But nobody here is complaining. Once the premier ski resort of France, Megève has been superseded by the scale and high technology of centres like nearby Trois Vallées and Tignes-Val d'Isère. Over the past three decades it has watched its standing reduced to that of tired old-timer – a resort, they say, for crusty Paris establishment types who don't really ski. Les Fermes de Marie has breathed some badly needed new life into the place.

Now it's a popular destination with vibrant, successful people from the worlds of music, the media and business, people who previously would have considered Megève not a place to escape to but from.

This is not all down to the charm of authentically weathered timber. The Sibuets have managed to strike that deeply seductive balance of exquisite design, luxury and faultless service on which a certain kind of traveller is increasingly willing to spend money. It seems that the less free time we have, the less compromises we are prepared to make when we spend it. The newly discerning traveller will not give up the massage centre, the sumptuous bedroom, the heated indoor pool, the fitness centre or the superb food just in order to ski.

The most demanding hedonist could not fault this place. A typical day at Les Fermes de Marie leaves you hard-pressed to find time for skiing. Breakfast starts the day in the vaulted, painted space of the converted cellars. Mid-morning cake and coffee (a Savoyard version of the traditional Austrian *Kaffee und Kuchen*) are served in a cosy panelled anteroom. After that there is just time for a swim in the indoor pool, housed in its own massive timber barn with a view of the slopes of Megève, before lunch in the soaring double-height space of the Gastronomic Restaurant; or if you prefer some sun you can eat on the deck by the traditional Savoyard cheese restaurant. An afternoon ski can be arranged in a jiffy: one of the hotel Land Rovers will take you to a lift station fully equipped with all the gear. Depending on the weather and your enthusiasm, you can ask to be collected in time for afternoon tea or arrange to have a post-ski massage. And then of course there's dinner. The food is of such a standard that Les Fermes de Marie's restaurant has become *the* place to eat in Megève.

The skiing may be no match for other purpose-built resorts, but the lifestyle is very difficult to beat. And anyway, should you find yourself in the mood for death-defying feats, Chamonix is only down the road.

---

address Les Fermes de Marie, Chemin de Riante Colline, 74120 Megève, France

telephone (33) 4 50 93 03 10   **fax** (39) 4 50 93 09 84

room rates from FF 1020

villa gallici

For well over a century the south of France has been a powerful magnet for those dreaming of escape. But parading along the Côte d'Azur in a skimpy bathing suit is not everybody's idea of the perfect getaway. For some, the culture of the Midi is as much of a drawcard as the beaches and the weather. If strolling through the immaculately preserved eighteenth-century Cours Mirabeau in Aix-en-Provence wearing black linen instead of black Lycra is more your style, then Villa Gallici is for you. An Italianate villa perched on a hill just a short walk from the historic city centre, Villa Gallici is perfectly positioned to enable you to experience one of the most beautiful cities in southern Europe.

Gallici gets its name from the original owner of the villa who, despite years of constant pressure to sell, refused to part with his beloved home – even though it was too much for the widower to manage. Eventually the team of Gil Dez and Charles Montemarco did convince him, but they kept the name as a tribute to old Monsieur Gallici. The Italianate architecture is a reminder that this part of France at one time belonged to Italy, but the interior is pure Provence. The tall armoires once filled with the family linen, the rusticated Louis XV and Louis XVI chairs with seats of woven rush, and the brightly colourful *Indiennes du Sud*, the patterned cottons originally made in imitation of fabrics from the Orient, are all unmistakably Provençal.

This cosy, cluttered and colourful style, familiar from countless coffee-table books, is what Gallici is all about. As a guest one thing is certain: you won't be bored with your room. There are yellow rooms, blue rooms, green rooms, ochre rooms, pink rooms … and each is decorated to extravagant perfection in a style dubbed 'provincial boudoir fantasy' by *Travel and Leisure* magazine. A truly extraordinary degree of attention has been lavished on every detail of Gallici's interiors, from the fabrics to the antiques, and it is matched by almost impossibly meticulous housekeeping and twenty-four-hour room service. It comes as no surprise that the proprietors made their mark as interior designers before launching into the hotel business. They had always travelled extensively for their work, and it was, they say, their wide experience of hotels that inspired their decision to open their own.

This being France, the food at Gallici gets as much attention as the design. From April to October, breakfast, lunch and dinner are served outdoors on the tree-lined terrace.

The sumptuous interiors were the creation of co-proprietors Gil Dez and Charles Montemarco

An Italianate mansion on the outskirts of Aix-en-Provence, Villa Gallici is only a five-minute stroll from the old town

The classical detailing at Villa Gallici is an appropriate reference to this town's history as an ancient Roman spa

The quality of light around Aix, hometown of Cézanne, has inspired many of the world's greatest artists

The decorative approach is unmistakably French and completely in the traditional style of Provence

An Italianate fountain decorates the terrace that serves as an outdoor dining room in summer

Charles Montemarco is particularly proud of the cuisine. As he will tell you, the traditional high standards of Provençal cooking are widely slipping. Gallici's chef prepares typical Provençal dishes such as *soupe de pistou*, *ratatouille*, and *tartelette aux tomates*. According to Montemarco, these need a true native with many years of experience to get right. Here they are superb, good enough to have earned Gallici's restaurant a reputation as one of the best in Aix.

Aix-en-Provence is an old Roman town that has been blessed with a gentle but impressive history. Its thermal springs, believed to have restorative powers, have been attracting visitors for two thousand years. It was also the city of Cézanne, and his work can be viewed at the Musée Granet as well as at his former studio, which is now open to the public. Each year in July, there is also the world-famous Aix Music Festival. Thus it's with good reason that *Condé Nast Traveller* magazine judged Aix 'probably the most civilized city in the world'.

The beauty, elegance and civility of Aix are often attributed to the fifteenth-century legacy of Good King René – poet, mathematician, planter of vineyards and patron of the arts, a ruler generally agreed to have been wise as well as a *bon vivant*. How very French, you might say; but in fact Aix is the way it is because it long resisted becoming fully French. It had its own parliament and court system until 1771, and even today the city court of appeals is second only to Paris in the number of cases it handles.

Probably the most enchanting feature of Villa Gallici is its location, the perfect distance from the heart of the old town for an after-dinner stroll. My favourites are the Place des Trois-Ormeaux, a small fountain square shaded by young elms, and the café Les Deux Garçons, the old haunt of Cézanne and Picasso. The fountains and the cafés are the real attraction of Aix, and attempting to make eye contact still the favourite distraction. No wonder Aix was also recently voted the sexiest city in France.

address Villa Gallici, avenue de la Violette, Impasse des Grands Pins, 13100 Aix-en-Provence, France

telephone (33) 4 42 23 29 23 **fax** (39) 4 42 96 30 45

room rates from FF 1350

babington house

'Of all the great things that the English have invented and made part of the credit of the national character, the most perfect, the most characteristic, the only one they have mastered completely in all its details so that it becomes a compendious illustration of their social genius and their manners, is the well-appointed, well-administered, well-filled country house.' So thought Henry James, and it's difficult not to agree. There's a romantic fantasy that pervades the English country house – an irresistible combination of nature, history and style. Sloshing through windswept fields in rubber boots; coming home to a roaring fire and a game of billiards … the invigorating pleasures of outdoor sports are perfectly complemented by the cosy comforts indoors.

Babington is an English country estate, and a Georgian one at that – the style that has not only become the most enduring signature of English architecture but is far and away the most covetable. Babington is a particularly beautiful example; in fact it may be the perfect English country house – not least because someone else launders the sheets and tidies up the mess. At Babington it is as it used to be: live like a lord and let someone else take care of the chores. But thankfully the food is not as

it used to be. Instead of 'roast something or other and one vegetable' Babington brings the urban food culture of London to the country. It must be the only country estate with a wood-fired oven (producing delicious home-made pizzas) and an industrial strength cappuccino machine.

Babington is equally adventurous in its approach to the interior. Tradition has been abandoned, and with great flair. The design signature shows a very healthy disrespect for frumpy chintz and family antiques. Modern and Georgian complement one another well, as no one who has been to Babington would dispute. Cynics might respond that this is a country house for people who don't really like the countryside, but if you have ever endured the 'romance' of a few nights in the country without modern comforts such as central heating, plenty of hot water and decent coffee, you would know that it is not romantic … just uncomfortable. The reality is that these stylish Georgian boxes demand an awful lot of maintenance and obscene amounts of money to heat properly. So the idea of running a country house as a club is rather ingenious. The old dining room is now a funky bar, and there are two restaurants and a fifty-seater cinema.

The bedrooms are sumptuously equipped with bathrooms that feature showers big enough for two and claw-foot baths that stand before marble fireplaces.

Yet all of this pales beside what has been accomplished with a bunch of old barns. The Cowshed, Babington's fitness centre, has a juice bar, a dance studio, a cardio training room and two swimming pools – both heated, both open all year round, one outside and one inside. A cold winter's day takes on new meaning when you start it with a swim through rising steam in an outdoor pool nestling among cow fields.

But none of these city-slicker luxuries takes anything away from the authenticity of the house and the surroundings. Set in fifteen acres of grounds, Babington is a genuine country estate that has always been a community unto itself. It still has its own picturesque chapel set at the end of an elegant tree-lined drive. Babington was first documented in the 1370s, and the seven-bay facade that gives the building its Georgian signature was not added until 1702. The house is in fact anything but pure Georgian. Ornate moulded ceilings are Queen Anne in period and style and the staircase is distinguished by a superb fifteenth-century stained-glass window. The dominant view from the interior is defined by a series of man-made lakes that cascade into one another; cherry blossom marks the arrival of spring; and immaculate lawns, dotted with old oaks, spread in every direction with not a hint of a road, building or telegraph pole to spoil the Arcadian scene.

Gardens, architecture, historical pedigree … Babington has it all, including the most essential ingredient of any successful country house, an interesting guest list. As the country counterpart of Soho House, London's most fashionable club, Babington mixes the elite from the worlds of film, television, radio and art with paying non-members, creating a laid-back atmosphere charged with a very English potential for scandal.

address Babington House, near Frome, Somerset, BA11 3RW, Great Britain

telephone (44) 1373 812266 **fax** (44) 1373 812112

room rates from UK £175

charlton house

Roger and Monty Saul, proprietors of Charlton House, know a thing or two about English country life. In fact they built a business empire around it. The fine leather and fashion goods label Mulberry epitomizes what is so attractive about the style we perceive as quintessentially English. Understated yet sophisticated, luxurious without being too grand, this is a style with the emphasis on comfort, quality of ingredients, craftsmanship, and a certain sophistication. It applies to − or at least used to apply to − British cars, houses and clothing. Think Jaguars, Aston Martins, Savile Row tailoring, Georgian architecture, handmade shoes: they all evoke a way of life concerned with elegance and prestige without compromising comfort. This 'quiet quality' was the foundation of the Sauls' approach to the design and manufacture of travel luggage and fashion. And inevitably, given the ever-increasing demand for home design, Mulberry's quintessentially English image came to be applied to a range for the home.

Charlton House, a historic Elizabethan manor in the Somerset town of Shepton Mallet, is a striking three-dimensional advertisement for the Mulberry line. It is a showcase of classically rich and romantic English style.

The property itself was first mentioned in the Domesday Book in the eleventh century. Many additions and restorations have been made since then: the porch is Victorian, the facade Georgian, the north front Elizabethan, and the east wall probably contemporary with Henry VIII.

But history and good looks are only one reason for escaping to Charlton House. For its most powerful draw is its food. Not so long ago you would have been tempting ridicule to suggest that a trip into the English countryside could be justified purely by the promise of good food. Even the most devoted Anglophile would have been hard-pressed to name rural retreats that could compete with the culinary inventiveness and quality of their counterparts in France. But the food culture of the English shires is evolving fast. London is no longer the dumb cousin of Paris when it comes to eating out, and the capital's thriving food scene has spread much further afield. Charlton House even has a Michelin star to prove it. Perhaps because of past prejudice, perhaps simply because the *Guide Michelin* is, after all, a French publication, it is not so unreasonable to suggest that such an accolade is even more of an achievement in England.

A fountain in front of Charlton House, which is renowned for its fine gardens

Military portraits in gilded frames are an essential ingredient in the English country estate look

The gardens are adorned with peculiarly English statuary, including these antique stone pineapples

The character of the bedrooms – all different – owes a lot to the hotel's collection of antique four-poster beds

Charlton House creates that 'polo in the country' feel with not a pony in sight

Breakfast and lunch are served in the conservatory. The hotel's restaurant has earned a Michelin star

So what exactly is so impressive about the food? First and foremost I'd have to say its consistency. For once breakfast, lunch and dinner are given equal billing in terms of choice, inventiveness and quality. So often only one slot receives all the attention, with breakfast relegated to a self-service buffet. Not so at Charlton.

Then there is head chef Adam Fellows, who certainly has all the right credentials. Trained by the Roux brothers at London's Le Gavroche, he also brings to the job the experience of cooking in a Brussels restaurant specializing in seafood. The Belgians take food very seriously indeed – which may be why Charlton House has become one of the best places to eat fish in England. The red mullet cooked with baby artichokes and spring onions is as far away from greasy fish and chips as you can get.

In between such gastronomic pleasures there's the benefit of simply being in the unspoilt Somerset countryside. Charlton has a tennis court, an indoor swimming pool and, as can be expected of a fine English estate, an exquisite garden complete with orchards, waterfalls, topiary, lawns and afternoon tea on the terrace. The historic towns of Bath and Wells are within easy daytripping distance, and on rainy days staying indoors is not such a bad prospect either. Charlton is the perfect complement to the recent vogue for Elizabethan period drama – a bit like a hotel version of *Shakespeare in Love*. I'm normally no fan of Elizabethan style, but I will admit that those chunky four-poster beds and all that embroidered silk, velvet and velour are very sexy. The combination of genuine Elizabethan and Tudor antiques with plush textiles in deep rich colours creates a romantic atmosphere that probably has little to do with Elizabethan reality and everything to do with romantic fantasy – a fantasy that you can live instead of just watching. It worked for Gwyneth Paltrow, and it certainly works for Charlton House.

address Charlton House, Shepton Mallet, near Bath, Somerset, BA4 4PR Great Britain
telephone (44) 1749 342008   **fax** (44) 1749 346362
room rates from UK £135

hotel tresanton

'Fish, tin and copper' goes the famous Cornish drinking toast – because until relatively recently, this southwestern tip of England was a hardy area that earned its living by fishing pilchards and mining tin and copper.

Life was hard, survival all-consuming. Its location gave Cornwall military importance (it was from here that the English defeated the mighty Spanish Armada) but in peacetime Cornwall was the forgotten corner of England. Before the industrial revolution and the rail network, the journey to the Cornish peninsula from London would average forty-eight hours. Thus, apart from a few strategic forts such as the castle at St Mawes and the odd private estate built from mining wealth, it was always an isolated, humble part of England with its own language and its own traditions.

In a bitter twist, life got even grimmer in the late nineteenth century, when the great schools of pilchards that the fishermen relied on stopped migrating past the Cornish coast. At the same time the expansion of empire led to the discovery of far greater and more accessible sources of tin and copper. Thus the two main industries of Cornwall collapsed almost simultaneously. An already tough life became almost unsustainable.

It was because times were so bad for so long that Cornwall stayed the same while the rest of Britain changed at breakneck speed. Its quaint fishing villages, idyllic harbours, white sandy beaches and rolling countryside are all intact. And therein lies the main reason why Cornwall is today considered the Riviera of the British Isles: no industry, no people – it's that simple. That, and the weather. By courtesy of the Gulf Stream, Cornwall has the most moderate climate in the British Isles. With a frost once in ten years, it's the only place tropical plants will survive at such northern latitudes. The whole of Cornwall, and the southern tip in particular, has a microclimate in which the temperature is usually several degrees higher than the rest of Britain. But the tag Riviera doesn't just refer to the unspoilt beauty and the balmy climate. It's also an indicator of price. So popular is Cornwall today that property prices are almost as high as in London and little thatched cottages in seaside villages almost never come on the market.

Olga Polizzi knows this area well. Her husband's family has had a holiday home on the bay of St Mawes for years. The Tresanton, a few doors down, was first opened in the late forties by her husband's godfather, Jack Siley.

St Mawes castle was built by Henry VIII to safeguard England's south coast

Hotel Tresanton has redefined the English seaside vacation: fewer frilly bits, more style

St Mawes is the perfect picturesque fishing village – a Cornish cliché come true

Each room is different – what they have in common is a simple pared-down sophistication

The dining room combines classic fifties Race chairs with tongue-and-groove panelling

The games room adjacent to the bar has sweeping views of the bay of St Mawes

The chef, like the table setting, is urban: Jock Zonfrillo has worked with Marco Pierre White and Gordon Ramsay

The main salon combines a massive open fireplace with floppy sofas and the odd scattering of antiques

Bathrooms look like they belong on a yacht, all pristine and panelled

The rooms at the front are typical of a Cornish country cottage

Despite a laid-back ambience, the food and service are impeccable: no buffet breakfast at Tresanton

The nautical theme is reinforced in the espresso bar by a compass motif in the mosaic tiled floor

Mosaic medallions decorate the dining-room floor

Olga Polizzi's design approach is bright and modern but comfortable

The idyllic bay of St Mawes is a popular place for yachting in the summer

The adjacent gardens were created by a New Zealander, who imported many of the exotic plants from down under

A microclimate created by the Gulf Stream allows some unlikely species to flourish in the subtropical gardens

An urban design signature contrasts successfully with the cosy cottage architecture of Cornwall

In its heyday it was one of the smartest hotels in Cornwall. But with the advent of affordable international travel in the seventies it went into a slow, gradual decline. 'Each time,' recalls Polizzi, 'that my husband and I would stay at the Anchorage we'd walk past Tresanton and he'd say "you ought to buy it and rescue it" … I toyed with the idea for years.'

Her temptation is understandable. As the daughter of Lord Forte, she has hotels in the blood. For most of her working life she has worked alongside her brother, Sir Rocco Forte, taking charge of building and design for such family jewels as the Eden in Rome, the George V in Paris and the Waldorf in London. Then in 1995 the Granada group staged a hostile takeover coup and seized control of the family business. This was her opportunity to realize a hotel of her own. The Tresanton, by then a tired affair teetering on the edge of collapse, had the potential; Polizzi had the time, the expertise and (after Granada's buyout) the money.

The result redefines the English seaside holiday. It brings style to Cornwall, as well as a restaurant on a par with London's best. Chef Jock Zonfrillo, a Scottish Italian, learned to cook with Marco Pierre White and Gordon Ramsay. The hotel is distinguished by what one London magazine described as 'a robust absence of prissiness'. There are no paper doilies, no mini-bars and not a floral print in sight. Instead the interior is all gleaming wooden floors, painted tongue-and-groove panelling and the odd antique – like a boat, simple and buttoned-down.

Despite its quickly gained reputation as the most stylish little English hotel outside London, Tresanton remains a family affair. Polizzi often pops in to lend a hand when the hotel is short-staffed, and her two daughters, Alex and Charlie, can be found slogging away in the restaurant for twelve hours at a stint. Even her husband, writer and biographer William Shawcross, occasionally gets to lug guests' baggage to their rooms.

address Hotel Tresanton, Lower Castle Road, St Mawes, TR2 5DR, Great Britain

telephone (44) 1326 270055 **fax** (44) 1326 270053

room rates from UK £220

mandawa desert resort

At first glance, this collection of mud huts in the arid wasteland of the Rajasthani desert might not seem a place one would spend time by choice. Yet it may be one of the most fascinating experiences that contemporary India has to offer.

Designed by the talented architectural duo Revathi and Kamath Singh from Delhi, the Mandawa Desert Resort was created to introduce the traveller to the simplicity and beauty of the native culture of India, without denying them the comforts that Westerners have come to expect. Revathi and Kamath are particular enthusiasts for building in mud, a material that in Rajasthan is both environmentally friendly and culturally appropriate. The huts of the resort camp, representing the homes of the village farmer, potter and weaver, are arranged to resemble a street in a traditional Rajasthani village. On the outside they are rendered in mud with white detailing. On the inside they reveal beautifully (but simply) appointed suites adorned with traditional Indian artifacts and richly coloured handwoven silks, and fitted with earthly comforts such as individual bathrooms elaborately constructed from local stone. Mandawa is undoubtedly one of the most

exotic hotels on the planet, and its strength is that it *wasn't* designed to be exotic, it was designed to be authentic.

The whole project started when the Thakur of Mandawa, a high-ranking member of the local nobility, approached the Singhs for help with a new project he was planning. Already a successful hotelier following the conversion of his city palace to a hotel, he now wanted to develop another hotel on a stretch of desert he owned just outside the town of Mandawa. He had with him a picture of what he envisaged – a photograph of a Canadian motel. Horrified at the prospect of such an inappropriate structure, but nonetheless intrigued by the possibilities and challenges of the project, Revathi and Kamath Singh embarked on a vigorous campaign to convince the Thakur not only of the merits of designing a hotel true to local aesthetics but, even more radically, of the idea of building in mud. Thankfully they succeeded, and what might have been an American-style motel became a traditional Rajasthani mud village carefully tailored to Western needs.

The Mandawa Desert Resort envelops you in a wealth of texture, colour and decorative detail – a powerful mix designed to evoke the symbolism of an ancient tribal village.

The point is to make you, the guest, take notice of the rich but simple way in which the local villagers have traditionally lived. If all this sounds too museum-ish, take heart from the fact that the camp is also handsome (in an ethnic sort of way) and very comfortable. Yes it is a carefully staged cultural experience, but not one that exacts the slightest measure of effort or sacrifice from the participant. All the senses, not just the visual, are catered to. There are large, cool, elaborate spaces in which to enjoy traditional Indian cuisine. This is predominantly vegetarian and bears no resemblance to the fare served in an average Indian restaurant in the West. There is a pool for those who want to cool off from the desert heat. The rooms are air-conditioned, and the camp is still close enough to the village of Mandawa for shopping and mingling in its more frenetic atmosphere.

Throughout the Mandawa Desert Resort the age-old tribal tradition of painting the surrounds of doors and windows with ornamental Sanskrit texts is continued in an annual ritual of renewal. Each year the monsoon washes away the mud render from the walls, and at the end of the rains the buildings are freshly rendered and repainted by village women. The purpose of the ornamentation is talismanic as well as decorative, for it is believed to have sacred and protective properties.

Needless to say, since its inauguration a little over a decade ago, the Mandawa Desert Resort has proven an extraordinary success. For beyond its cultural interest it also offers qualities that are almost impossible to find in India – peace, quiet and genuine isolation. As such it represents a rare respite from the great tide of hectic humanity that threatens to engulf you everywhere else. It will hardly come as a surprise that most Indians don't live in palaces, yet neither do most travellers ever really get a taste of how life has traditionally been lived on this extraordinary subcontinent. Here is your chance.

address The Desert Resort Mandawa, District Jhunjhunu, Shekhawati, Rajasthan 333 704, India

telephone (91) 1592 231 51   **fax** (91) 1592 231 71

room rates from Rs 1550

neemrana fort-palace

There is no shortage of palaces in India, particularly in the state of Rajasthan, but none, in my opinion, conveys the grandeur and refinement of India's aristocracy more powerfully than Neemrana.

Throughout its long history, right up until independence in 1947, the Indian subcontinent was divided into hundreds of individual fiefdoms, each under the absolute rule of a hereditary prince or maharaja. Even the British, during the centuries of colonial rule, maintained the maharajas on their individual thrones: this was the only practicable way to govern what had, since the time of Alexander the Great, been considered an 'ungovernable nation'. In a gentlemanly deal with the devil, the maharajas were allowed to keep their wealth and local positions provided they did the bidding of their colonial overlords – a deal backed up by the bureaucratic and military might of the British Empire.

Neemrana was built as a fortified palace for the maharaja of Neemrana in 1464. It remained the family seat until 1947, when the last maharaja, Rajandra Singh, a man ahead of his time, voluntarily moved out of the palace in prescient anticipation of the coming abolition of all royal privileges. For the next three

decades, the local villagers, emboldened by social revolution, proceeded to treat the abandoned palace as a handy supply of building materials. In the process they stripped the magnificent structure down to a threadbare shadow of its former self. The doors, windows, even the stone floors were ransacked. All that remained when the present proprietors laid eyes on it in 1978 was 'a splendid ruin'.

The task of renovation that confronted them was one of monumental scope and proportion. Aman Nath, an Indian historian and author; O.P. Jain, the proprietor of a business that finds and restores antique Indian furniture; Lekha Poddar, a member of one of India's leading industrialist families; and Francis Wacziarg, a Delhi-based Frenchman who exports a variety of Indian craft to the likes of Habitat and Ikea, together set about rebuilding the dilapidated pile that had once been the headquarters of the Hindu Chauhan dynasty. In the absence of historical records or photographs they were guided simply by traditional norms and techniques. This was a project of blind courage and unwavering commitment. Much to their credit, the result, in the well-deserved words of Aman Nath, is 'better than it ever was in its heyday'.

As palaces go, particularly in Rajasthan, Neemrana is neither the most famous nor the most spectacular. Udaipur's Lake Palace, for example, is more enchanting ... at least from a distance. But up close you realize that the interior spaces have been sacrificed to the conventional norms of a Hilton or a Sheraton. Lobbies, restaurants and box-like guest rooms have replaced the original labyrinthine arrangement of sweeping halls and grand, sparsely furnished chambers.

Not so with Neemrana. The rambling old fort has retained all of its original spatial complexity. It still has its myriad of hidden courtyards, secret corridors, stairways and terraces that make it such a riveting and exotic experience. Unlike most converted palaces, Neemrana was not an exercise in squeezing the maximum number of rooms out of the available space. Despite the massive size of the structure, the planning provided for only thirty-odd guest suites; each one different and each of a scale and complexity that is true to the original spirit of the place. In terms of decoration these suites reflect a dignified approach that is perfectly appropriate not only to the heritage of the building but also to the intense heat of the Rajasthani desert.

The fort is built into a steep hill overlooking the village of Neemrana, two hours from Delhi by car but centuries away in atmosphere. Villagers go about their lives in timeless fashion, and there is a peace and tranquillity here that is ever more difficult to find in India. This is a fact obviously not lost on the various ambassadors who have made it their regular weekend escape from the noise, pollution and sheer mass of humanity of Delhi.

Here on the edge of the Rajasthani desert the temperature drops after sundown like a brick, which not only makes for comfortable nights but also clads the fort in an eerie early morning mist that is a delight to wake up to. Once upon a time the inhabitants of Neemrana Fort-Palace lived simply, amid great splendour ... nothing has changed.

address Neemrana Fort-Palace, Village Neemrana, District Alwar, Rajasthan - 301705, India

telephone (91) 11 461 6145 **fax** (91) 11 462 1112

room rates from Rs 1500

surya samudra

Situated on a rocky promontory between two deserted beaches, Surya Samudra is the kind of place you could easily imagine Hemingway or Somerset Maugham retreating to for weeks at a time to bash away at a typewriter in splendid isolation. The state of Kerala, along India's southwest coast, certainly bears no resemblance to the arid north. With its endless coconut groves swaying in the tropical breeze and its countless empty white beaches, not to mention a sensuous, laid-back way of life, it is a perfect retreat from the heady experience of so much of India.

Surya Samudra began as a single octagonal stone house thirty miles from the tip of the subcontinent and just a few minutes from the historic Vizhinjam harbour. The site and its development potential were first pointed out to German professor Klaus Schleusener two decades ago by a local who clearly possessed some insight. Schleusener didn't hesitate for a moment. He originally came here to teach at the Indian Institute of Technology at Madras as part of an Indian–German cultural exchange programme, but before long found (as so many do) that the country had got into his blood. So he bought the land with the help of Indian friends and proceeded to design a retreat entirely attuned to the setting, the climate and the local traditions of Kerala.

The octagonal shape was chosen to allow as many faces as possible to open onto the extraordinary view. The space, particularly its ceiling height, was calculated to counter the heat, while stone was chosen as the building material for its robust and insulating properties. Doors and windows were installed only so that the property could be secured, as well as to protect the interior from the driving rains of the monsoon. Most of the time the house is entirely open to the breeze. Furnishings are limited to basic essentials in natural materials: stone, terracotta tiles, whitewashed granite and recycled wooden beams.

A lot of lessons were learned from the local vernacular architecture. Houses in Kerala are traditionally built in a durable hardwood similar to teak, with thatched or tiled roofs and large cutout openings onto shaded verandas. Schleusener's study of traditional south Indian architecture inspired in him a passionate interest in the style and the area. His own house was the perfect place from which to indulge that passion. At night he would organize concerts of traditional dance, or music played on sitar, drums and flute.

Breezy and cool, the interiors – in dark wood with the odd bit of raw silk – are perfect for Kerala's hot, sticky climate

Almost on the southern tip of India, Surya Samudra's cottages overlook two beaches visited only by local fishermen

Ancient trade routes carried the influence of southern India's architecture far into Southeast Asia

Kerala, India's southernmost state, is lush and tropical, unlike the arid north

The owner's octagonal cottage – a piece of Hindu minimalism – enjoys the best view of all and is now part of the resort

The traditional cottages were rescued from demolition, dismantled, and reassembled overlooking the ocean

By day he travelled the back roads of Kerala, forever on a mission to save just one more piece of indigenous architecture from imminent destruction.

Like most people with their own slice of paradise, it was never really Schleusener's intention to share. But being unable to resist last-minute rescues (he would buy properties from locals who were just about to tear them down) he ended up with quite a collection of wooden houses, all with their original carvings. These represent a tradition that influenced the architecture of all of Southeast and East Asia, as far away as Japan. Painstakingly dismantled, each one was reconstructed, piece by numbered piece, looking out over the Indian Ocean. The original intention was that they should serve as accommodation for friends and family. By the time he had twelve houses, he found he had too many 'friends', and the decision to open to paying guests came as a natural progression. Little changed in this transition, apart from the recent addition of

a pool carved out of the granite rock. There are still performances of classical dance and martial arts, and the houses all preserve their traditional form, save for the addition of 'bathgardens' built as annexes open to the sky at the back of each structure.

But there is one major surprise, perhaps previously a jealously guarded family secret: the food. During the monsoon months (June and July) Klaus heads to his other house on Italy's Lake Como, and over the years he has taken some of the kitchen staff with him to be trained in European cuisine. This must have been a potent learning experience because every chance they get, the Surya Samudra chefs want to impress you with their skills. Ask for afternoon tea and their eyes light up at the opportunity to bake yet another cake. At night freshly caught fish is prepared with Italian herbs accompanied by Indian-style vegetables.

A teak shack on the beach, Italian cooking in the tropics and good karma – what more could any sensible human being want?

address Surya Samudra Beach Garden, Pulinkudi, Mullur PO, Thiruvananthapuram 695 521, Kerala, India

telephone (91) 471 480 413 **fax** (91) 471 481 124

room rates from Rs 4500

atelier sul mare

Sicily has been a hub of civilization since the earliest days of Mediterranean history. Egyptian, Phoenician, Roman and Greek empires have used the conveniently located island as a foothold in conducting trade around the region. Once virtually a colony of ancient Greece, Sicily has been a stomping ground for European culture for three thousand years. Two hundred years ago Nelson parked the collective might of the British fleet in the bay of Palermo and was reluctant to leave, and just over a century ago Garibaldi led his Red Shirts to an astounding coup, ending the Bourbon iron grip over southern Italy and paving the way for the first unification of the Italian peninsula since Roman times.

It's perhaps fitting that an island with so much history should play host to such a modern phenomenon as Atelier sul Mare. Founded by entrepreneur Antonio Presti, son of a local cement magnate, Atelier sul Mare is this Sicilian businessman's second major project patronizing modern art on a monumental scale. The first was Fiumara d'Arte – 'Art Stream' – a sculpture park that features the commissioned work of nine international contemporary artists. The spectacular works are each the size of two- and three-storey buildings and wind along the course of the River Tusa in the Nebrodi Mountains Park of northeast Sicily.

Presti's campaign to bring art to this forgotten corner of Sicily was followed by Atelier sul Mare, a hotel that introduces the idea of living with art. Unlike the famous Colombe d'Or in the south of France, which is decorated with a collection of works by some of the world's greatest modern artists, at Atelier sul Mare artists were invited to each turn an entire guest room into an art installation. With the only two restrictions being that there had to be somewhere to hang clothes and a mattress to sleep on, the artists (many of whom also participated in the Fiumara d'Arte) were restricted only by their imaginations. One contributor, Chilean film director Raoul Ruiz, conjured a minimalist planetarium: a thirty-foot circular black tower with a revolving round bed at the base and a sliding roof that opens to the sky. Video-artist Fabrizio Plessi created a room called 'The Sea Denied' that is panelled on all sides with old doors to completely block all evidence of the hotel's seaside location ... except for a row of half a dozen video screens playing a tape of waves repeatedly crashing on a shore.

One room, conceived as a tribute to Italian poet and film director Pasolini, recreates the interior of a Yemeni hut

Located on Sicily's rocky northeast coast, Atelier sul Mare is literally on the water's edge

'Nest' by Paolo Icaro is a concrete-walled, oval-shaped sanctuary in which even the bedcover mimics feathers

'Energy' by Maurizio Mochetti is a red
and white glowing fantasy that entirely
shuts out the blue of the Mediterranean

Fourteen of the forty rooms were
designed by internationally
acknowledged contemporary artists

The bar, originally an old garage,
is decorated inside and out with
local graffiti art

But without a doubt the craziest room is the one created by Presti himself as a tribute to his hero, the Italian poet and film director Pier Paolo Pasolini. This entire room is covered wall to wall in red mud, in reference to Pasolini's favourite country, the Yemen. This has been inscribed with a graphic white border of Pasolini's words written in Arabic. Even the telephone is hidden under a mud-covered flap in the floor. But that's nothing compared to the bathroom. Called the Car Wash (because Pasolini died in a car accident), it's a spaghetti tangle of copper pipes that spring from the walls like snakes from the head of the Medusa and spray water in every conceivable direction. Children, predictably, absolutely love it.

And that, for Antonio Presti, is the point – to make art fun. He's convinced that art has been ruined by heavy-handed intellectuals and investment buyers. It dismays him that people are so rarely exposed to works of art and when they are it's in the stifling environment of a museum. So despite the fact that some of the artists involved have international reputations, this is not an elite project. Quite the opposite. It actually helps if you don't know much about modern art, for then you are free to experience the hotel with a totally open mind.

And that is certainly what happens every morning, in an unlikely ritual in which guests throw their keys into a large stone bowl on the reception desk and are then invited to grab a set and take themselves on a tour of the other rooms. It sounds like a formula for disastrous invasions of privacy – what about those forgotten underpants left hanging in the bathroom? But because the management is relaxed about it, so is everyone else.

Not one aspect of Atelier sul Mare accords with convention. The bar is a graffiti-painted garage, while the lobby contains a monumental kiln in which guests can fire their own crockery designs (there is, as a result, not a matching cup and saucer on site). It all expresses the delightfully twisted imagination of proprietor Antonio Presti.

address Atelier sul Mare, via Cesare Battisti 4, Castel di Tusa, Messina, Sicily, Italy
telephone (39) 0921 334295 **fax** (39) 0921 334283
room rates from L100,000

certosa di maggiano

The oldest surviving Carthusian monastery in Tuscany, Certosa di Maggiano was founded in 1316 by Cardinal Riccardo Petroni. Set in the rolling Tuscan hills outside Siena, it was originally home to twelve monks and a prior. These monks left more than their architecture; they also bequeathed their immaculate silence.

A prestigious architectural heritage was no assurance of immortality, however – far from it. When the present owners, a couple from Milan, first stumbled upon the complex it was a bewildering maze of add-on constructions and extensions, its architecture entirely disfigured by centuries of indifference. Anna Grossi Recordati was undeterred. She had relocated to Siena when her husband, a renowned cardiac surgeon, became dean of the city's centuries-old university. Despite the state of the building, she saw in this gigantic stone puzzle a potential home for her family. To realize her vision she enlisted the help of the late Renzo Mongiardino, Italy's most accomplished interior architect and a great authority on decorative history.

Under Mongiardino's expert eye, the original architecture, with columns in *pietra serena* and magnificent vaulted ceilings, was restored wherever possible. Where the cloisters were beyond redemption, exact replicas of the fourteenth-century originals were painstakingly built. Most importantly, and as a great credit to the vision and courage of the Grossis, the spirit of the monastery was revived. Today, the magnificent chapel that dominates the property is reserved for Sunday service and nothing more.

Over a decade after Mongiardino's work was completed, it still looks timeless. He was a successful hunter of the rare and the beautiful, and a firm favourite of Italy's richest and most powerful families, including the Agnellis. When it came to the decoration of Certosa di Maggiano, he invested in big, important pieces – no froufrou knick-knacks for him. The gilded chandelier that dominates and defines the winter dining room, for example, is a huge but simple Murano original, hung low from the vaulted ceiling to create maximum effect. The drawing room, known as the Emperor's Hall, is furnished with deep down-filled sofas upholstered in tea-stained chintz. The room is dominated by a series of twelve Venetian paintings depicting Roman emperors astride their favourite mounts. These are set directly onto the wall in *trompe l'oeil* frames.

The library exemplifies the soaring vaulted spaces of this fourteenth-century Carthusian monastery

Set on a vineyard-clad hill overlooking Siena, the view from Certosa di Maggiano is Tuscany perfected

Sumptuous fabrics and rich colours are the essence of the hotel's decorative style

Lunch is served under the carefully restored colonnades running alongside what is now the swimming pool

Thirty acres of gardens and vineyards surround the famous Renaissance monastery

Breakfast is served in the original kitchen of the monks' quarters

Above all, Mongiardino succeeded in domesticating the spaces without sacrificing their integrity. But eventually Signor Grossi's tenure in Siena came to a close, the children grew up, and the Grossis returned to Milan. Rather than abandon their creation, they decided to transform it into a small luxury hotel. Once again, Anna Grossi Recordati, together with her daughter (who runs the place today), was on a mission: if it was to be a hotel, it had to be a great hotel. It is – Certosa di Maggiano became a member of the prestigious Relais & Chateaux chain within two years of the decision to convert to a hotel.

It's easy to understand its instant popularity. The same qualities that seduced the Grossis a decade and a half earlier are equally irresistible to short-term visitors. Situated on a hilltop on the outskirts of the historic city of Siena, amid thirty acres of vineyards and gardens, it is everything we dream that Tuscany should be: historic, intoxicating, romantic, beautiful and quiet. Anyone who has ever holidayed in Italy will know that Italians, particularly young Italians, love anything with an engine, and they delight in zooming up and down the smallest village streets until the small hours – great fun for them, but a nightmare for us travellers. At Certosa you hear nothing. It really does feel like you have travelled back in time to the Tuscany that inspired D.H. Lawrence.

What is Italy, however, without the food? In the best tradition of Tuscany the food is simple and based on local produce, renowned for its quality. There are no superstar chefs in the kitchen and no tortured international 'hybrid' dishes on the menu. Breakfast is served in the original tiled kitchen (or on its adjoining terrace, depending on the weather), lunch is served in the shade of the vaulted arcade alongside a canal that fills the swimming pool, and dinner is taken in the original cloister. Almost seven hundred years ago, Certosa di Maggiano was built to be a retreat and a place of silence; it still is.

address Hotel Certosa di Maggiano, Strada di Certosa 82, 53100 Siena, Italy

telephone (39) 0 577 288 180   **fax** (39) 0 577 288 189

room rates from L700,000

il pellicano

Is this the most romantic retreat in Italy? Many people think so. The story of Il Pellicano is the story of two lovers, Michael Graham and Patsy Daszel. Graham was a dashing British pilot who captured the world's imagination with news of a daring escape from disaster. The sole survivor of an air crash in the African jungle, Graham jumped from the plane without a parachute, relying on the dense canopy below to break his fall. Patsy Daszel was a charismatic American beauty who was being courted by Clark Gable when the story of this extraordinary feat hit the world's headlines. Daszel was completely captivated and immediately wanted to meet this 'brave and lucky' man. As fate would have it she did, by accident, at a place in California called Pelican Point. It was love at first sight.

Il Pellicano was the result, many years later, of the couple's exhaustive search all over Europe for a romantic hideaway where they could relive their first encounter. They chose an inaccessible corner of Monte Argentario, a hundred miles northwest of Rome, which in the sixties was a haven of untamed nature: spectacular cliffs, clear azure water and dense forest. Connected to the mainland by just a couple of causeways, the mountain rises from the sea to a double peak. In those days it was mostly forested and uninhabited, and wholly unspoilt by noisy roads or large buildings – and it still is. Il Pellicano started as a villa that the lovers built for themselves, soon followed by several neighbouring villas for friends. It was officially opened as a hotel by Charlie Chaplin in 1965 and proved a big hit from the very first day, particularly with celebrities looking for simplicity and privacy in a sensational setting.

Consistently voted one of the best hotels in the world, the prevailing mood, as *Harpers & Queen* describes it, is 'a mixture of country club and house party'. It's a strangely seductive place, one that so quickly becomes familiar that you feel a sense of *déjà vu*. Despite being located around the corner from Porto Ercole, one of the most elite of Italy's summer communities, Il Pellicano is neither ostentatious nor glamorous. The lifestyle is easy and relaxed and the approach to the design and architecture one of discreet elegance.

Il Pellicano's real sophistication is in the things that you don't see. The private garage for instance, housing fifty-odd cars, was cut into the mountainside and hidden out of sight below the two artificial grass tennis courts.

Similarly, there is a lift carved into the cliff for those who are too lazy (or too relaxed) to take the winding steps back up from the seaside bathing platform to the cottages set further up the mountain. And despite the fact that you can't even see the neighbours, all the buildings on the property (six cottages and the main building housing reception, bar and restaurant) follow a strict code established for the area. External walls are all in the same shade of terracotta render and all roofs are covered in the clay tiles typical of Tuscan architecture.

The Spanish royal family, Leonard Bernstein and Gianni Agnelli are among the high-profile guests who have chosen to holiday here in the past, attracted by the absolute privacy Il Pellicano can offer. But if you're not a movie star and are after something more than lying in the sun in splendid isolation, the fact that you are in Italy adds another dimension. With its proximity to both Rome and central Tuscany, the Argentario offers access to an impressive variety of both Roman and Etruscan ruins, as well as magnificent forts left behind by the Spaniards who ruled here in the sixteenth and seventeenth centuries. In the days of ancient Rome the promontory belonged to a family of financiers (*argentarii* in Latin). One member of this family, Domitius Ahenobarbus, married Agrippina, sister of Caligula, and became the father of Nero. With such impressive connections it comes as no surprise that there are the ruins of five vast and luxurious Roman villas just on the Argentario itself, recorded by Julius Caesar in his *De Bello Civili*.

On a more contemporary (if less worthy) note, the shopping is not bad either. The old fortified harbour town of Porto Ercole is a pretty place to stroll, as are the old towns of nearby Porto Santo Stefano and Orbetello. There are boutiques worth visiting in all three, as well as local markets. You could even take a daytrip to inland Tuscany, have lunch in the beautiful medieval city of Siena, and be back in time for a late afternoon swim.

address Il Pellicano, 58018 Porto Ercole (GR), Italy

telephone (39) 0 564 833801   **fax** (39) 0 564 833418

room rates from L350,000

la posta vecchia

Is there anything more seductive than an Italian Renaissance palazzo in the summer? Probably not … except perhaps an Italian Renaissance palazzo on the beach. Surely this must be the ultimate. One of the century's most legendary rich men certainly thought so. Not so long ago, La Posta Vecchia was the primary residence of J. Paul Getty, as famous for his oil fortune as he was infamous for his penny-pinching ways.

One thing Getty never skimped on was his passion for architecture, art and antiquity. For centuries this impressive double-fronted palazzo, less than an hour from Rome, was the hereditary property of the Odescalchi family. Commissioned in 1640, it was built as a residential hotel for tradesmen and other visitors (the family lived in the fortified castle next door). It gained its name when it became one of the official stops for coaches carrying the royal mail. Getty was acquainted with the Odescalchis and had on occasion leased their castle for the summer. But it was the seventeenth-century structure next door that really caught his eye, despite its dilapidated state. Prince Ladislao Odescalchi was originally reluctant to sell, but Getty's indomitable will eventually prevailed, and in

1965 he purchased La Posta Vecchia together with a sizeable portion of land.

Getty immediately embarked on a full-scale renovation and, with the help of art historian Federico Zeri, began a decade-long quest to furnish the property with museum-quality paintings and antiques, particularly classical pieces, Getty's passion. But even his larger-than-life lust for the relics of Rome could not prepare him for the mother load that awaited here. Half-way through digging up the garden for a swimming pool, work had to stop. The labourers had uncovered the ruins of a significant Roman villa, said by some to have belonged to the Emperor Tiberius. Archaeologists were brought in, and a villa complete with a booty of amphorae and other ancient relics was uncovered.

Getty's heart was set on a pool (despite the property's private black-sand beach) so a new location was selected in the garden. But when digging started afresh, lo and behold … another villa. The archaeologists returned and work slowed to hand-brush pace. Never one to give up easily, Getty decided to build a pool complex underneath the house instead. Before they could begin, the entire palazzo had to be suspended on massive steel beams.

Tiramisu finished with a swirl of
peppermint is a speciality
of the kitchen

La Posta Vecchia is a Renaissance
Italian palazzo bang on the
Mediterranean coast

Every space, every corner is testament
to the most exquisite attention to
detail money could buy

The indoor swimming pool in one
of the palazzo's wings has a history
all of its own

When J. Paul Getty sold the palazzo in
1975, his cook stayed on. One of her
best dishes is pasta with scampi

Many of the bathrooms come complete
with magnificent marble fireplaces

A connecting corridor space serves
as a small private living area

The dining room occupies the opposite
wing to the one containing the
swimming pool

A solid marble bathtub complete with
bronze swan-shaped taps

The front of the palazzo is directly on the sea wall; to the rear it overlooks acres of formal classical gardens

To furnish the villa, Getty employed an art historian for the better part of a decade

A detail of the red velour antique bedhead in one of the guest rooms

Scagliola – polished marble inlaid with coloured lime mortar – on a table top in one of the reception spaces

Getty filled the house with priceless pieces that were sold with the property when he left

The bathroom in what was Getty's own suite is a masterpiece of solid pink marble overkill

The present owners have experimented for years to find exactly the right shade of terracotta for the external walls

Opulent, spacious, grand – the guest suites at La Posta Vecchia recall the days when this was a private palazzo

Getty was a firm fan of antiquity. The classical figures that decorate the corridors are of museum quality

When digging resumed, no prizes for guessing what they found! This villa was in significantly better condition, with its mosaic floors intact and enough artifacts to fill a museum. So that is exactly what Getty did: he turned the excavated space beneath the house into a private museum for his own hoard of Roman antiquities. As for the pool, Getty opted to build it in the one place where he could be guaranteed *not* to find a Roman villa – inside the house. An entire wing of the palazzo was given over to it.

For Getty the story didn't have a happy ending. In one of the century's most notorious kidnapping cases, the Brigate Rosse seized his grandson and cut off his ear to show they meant business. Getty paid the ransom, left Italy in disgust, and vowed never to return. He kept to his word. The palazzo and all its incredible contents were sold lock, stock and barrel to the Sciò family. They used it as a summer house until the kids grew up and they no longer needed the space. Had it not been for the enthusiasm of Roberto Sciò it might

have been sold. Instead, he convinced his family to turn La Posta Vecchia into a small luxury hotel, just as it was in the beginning.

Everything is as Getty left it: each chair, mirror, table or painting could be in a museum. Anywhere else this might be discomforting, but the Italians have an easy attitude towards their history – even when the bed in your room used to belong to Maria de' Medici. The cook first hired by Getty almost thirty years ago also came with the house. She continues to prepare a menu based on simplicity and freshness of ingredients. Nothing too complicated – the food is like the atmosphere, relaxed and informal. The emphasis is on fish and shellfish, as you might expect in a seaside location. From May to October, meals are served on the terrace overlooking the Mediterranean.

So if you ever wondered what it would be like to live like J. Paul Getty (minus the bodyguards and the permanent paranoia that everyone is after your money) then La Posta Vecchia is your chance … take it.

address La Posta Vecchia, 00055 Palo Laziale, Roma, Italy
telephone (39) 0 6 9949501   **fax** (39) 0 6 9949507
room rates from L775,000

parco dei principi

The Amalfi coast is one of Italy's most enduringly beautiful landscapes, a continuous strip of volcanic mountains that plunge into an emerald-green Mediterranean. The established haunt of writers, directors, film stars and royals, this is where Liz Taylor and Richard Burton escaped to for their torrid affair while filming *Cleopatra* in Rome, where American author and society wit Gore Vidal lives for several months a year, and where Franco Zeffirelli has entertained American film stars and British royalty alike.

The Amalfi coast combines the seductive climate and passion of the southern Mediterranean with a culture defined by almost three millennia of civilization. From the ancient Greeks to the Bourbon kings, this stretch south of Naples has been coveted by a non-stop succession of powerful rulers. Hence you will find Roman ruins (Pompeii and Herculaneum), Renaissance palazzi, Belle Epoque villas, medieval churches, and of course the timeless little fishing villages that appear on all the postcards. What you don't expect to find, perhaps because it seems so modern amid all this antiquity, is a masterpiece by Italy's most famous twentieth-century architect, Gio Ponti.

Ponti is to Italy what Frank Lloyd Wright is to America – a creative giant whose work shaped and redefined the aesthetic direction of a nation. Ponti designed Milan's landmark skyscraper, the famous Pirelli Building; he founded *Domus*, the world's most prestigious design and architecture magazine; and he designed ceramics and furniture for Italy's top factories. Although one automatically associates his work with a slick city environment like Milan, one of his most enduring projects and certainly one of his funkiest stands on the Amalfi coast. Hanging a few hundred metres above the sparkling Mediterranean on the edge of Sorrento's typically spectacular cliffs, Parco dei Principi is a testament to the timeless originality of Ponti's work. It is still as fresh and surprising and utterly stylish today as when it was completed more than thirty years ago.

For Parco dei Principi, Ponti designed every single element: the building, the furniture, the blinds, the wall decoration, the plates and even the tiles. As a result this hotel is a complete original ... a total one-off. There is simply nothing else like it in the world. Outside it's like a giant piece of white card with geometric cutouts; inside it resembles a huge, modernist beach cabana, all blue and white.

Gio Ponti had a thing about using a single colour – he believed it was the only way to approach interior design. For Parco dei Principi he chose a palette of blues. Glossy blue concrete eggs are embedded in white walls; Venetian blinds in different shades of blue form bold planes of horizontal stripes, lobby furniture is upholstered in navy blue wool, and even the telephones were specially commissioned in a particular shade of blue. But it was for the floors that Ponti really put his 'one colour' theory to the creative test. Working with a local tile manufacturer he designed numerous variations of geometric patterns in three different shades of blue with white. So mesmerizing are the floors that I was all prepared to photograph each and every pattern … until the management tactfully reminded me that Ponti had designed a hundred different tile patterns for Parco dei Principi. This, after all, is the Amalfi coast and there are better things to do than look at the floor all day.

From May to October this a hedonistic pleasure playground with few equals. It has the weather (hot and sunny), the people (slim, sexy and suntanned), and the food (a mix of dishes from Tuscany and the more spicy tomato-based cuisine of Calabria), not to mention the pizzas for which the Neapolitans are famous. Life is all about renting a scooter and zipping around the idyllic coastal roads, finding a little restaurant in a fishing village, and then diving into the sea after lunch. An elderly Belgian couple I met at the hotel had been coming to Parco dei Principi for a month every year for the past twenty years. When they first made the excursion from Belgium their daughter was just a baby; now she had dragged her boyfriend along, and they were sure they would eventually be bringing the grandchildren to continue the tradition. I doubt that they even knew who Gio Ponti was – what they loved about the hotel was the fact that it was still, after twenty years, the most stylish and original they had ever seen.

address   Hotel Parco dei Principi, Vita Rota 1, Sorrento, 80067, Italy

telephone (39) 0 81 878 2101   **fax** (39) 0 81 878 3786

room rates from L300,000

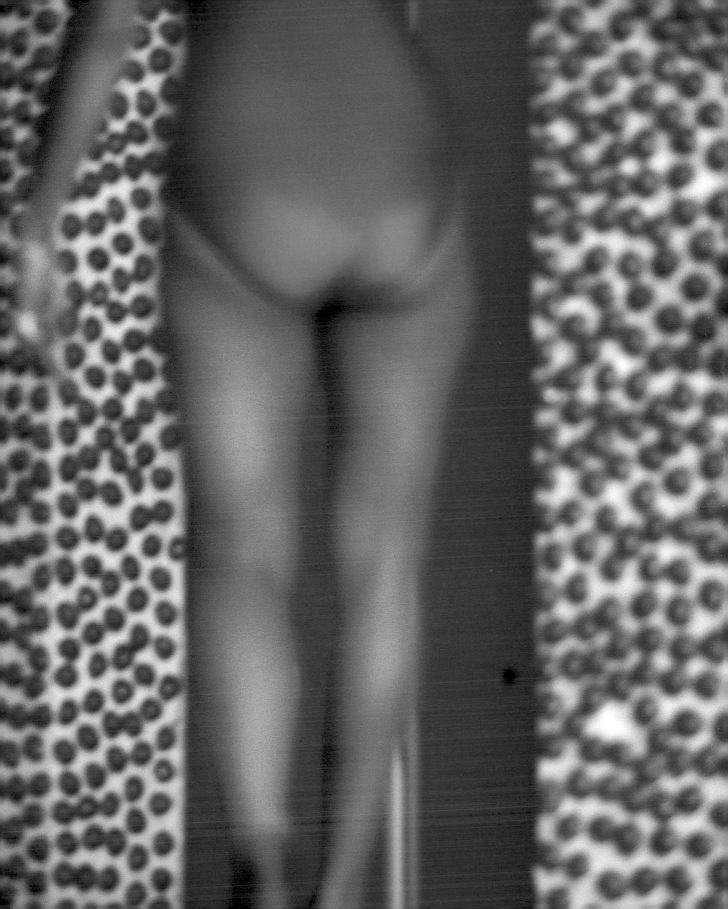

strawberry hill

Strawberry Hill is a former coffee plantation perched on a dark green plateau 3,100 feet above sea level in the midst of Jamaica's lush Blue Mountains. It looks down on the sprawling city of Kingston below and the blue-green waters of the Caribbean beyond. It once belonged to the Earl of Orford, a.k.a. Horace Walpole, who is reputed to have been deeded the rich twenty-six-acre estate by the British royal family late in the eighteenth century. So although strawberries were (and still are) grown on the property, the name was in fact taken from Walpole's Gothic-style estate in Twickenham, England.

It may be almost three hundred years since the plantation was set up, but remarkably little has changed. This may be largely due to its remoteness. Once upon a time the journey from Kingston to Strawberry Hill would be made in a horse-drawn carriage up a winding track. Today, the journey by car is not much quicker. The road is now paved, but it is just as steep, and the many hairpin bends make any real speed impossible.

Over the years the estate has changed hands many times, but the sophisticated colonial lifestyle has been preserved. Chris Blackwell, founder of Island Records, remembers going there for afternoon tea with his parents as a child, a longstanding tradition begun by the DaCosta family, proprietors of the plantation in the forties. Years later, in 1972, Blackwell purchased the property himself and throughout the eighties entertained many celebrities and famous musicians here, including the Rolling Stones and Bob Marley. Strawberry Hill, like its English namesake, became a salon of sorts, a place where people would get together informally over lunch in the cool, crisp mountain air. So it was a natural step to open it as a restaurant in 1986. The Great House, a single-storey timber structure in the Georgian style, was renovated for the purpose and duly won a National Heritage award for architecture.

Disaster struck just two years later in the form of Hurricane Gilbert. The two-hundred-year-old institution was obliterated in a matter of hours. Only in 1991 did Blackwell decide to build again, with a commission for a cottage from Jamaican architect Ann Hodges. This was a great success, a contemporary interpretation of the traditional Jamaican aesthetic. Blackwell subsequently called upon Hodges, together with local project manager Jonathan Surtees, to build others for family and friends.

From this, the idea evolved for an intimate mountainside hotel. Finally, in 1994, Blackwell opened Strawberry Hill, the first and original Island Outpost hotel in Jamaica.

The architecture and design of Strawberry Hill's twelve guest villas are stunning and truly deserving of all the many prizes they have earned to date. With their awnings, verandas and mountain vistas, they are apparently a self-contained world set well apart from local life. But in fact the biggest attraction here is that the place continues to play a role in Jamaican society. It is not just a luxurious retreat for overseas tourists; the excellent restaurant attached to the hotel is well known locally and Sunday brunch has become a regular fixture for politicians, artists, writers and other key members of Kingston's urban set, who make the forty-five-minute drive into the cool and misty Blue Mountains each week to eat, discuss and linger until sunset. The local element gives the place an edge, reclaiming it from the exclusivity of colonial tradition. So although the location is wonderfully remote, Strawberry Hill doesn't feel at all aloof from the vibrant urban culture of Kingston below.

But aside from the food, the truly spectacular location and the cool temperatures, Strawberry Hill is also renowned as a spa – an Aveda spa. The lush gardens and winding trails of the former plantation provide the perfect complement to the Aveda commitment to beauty and well-being. And make no mistake: this is a spa with serious facilities, not just a bunch of massage benches set up under a tree. An entirely separate building was purpose-built for the spa. The treatments on offer, normally administered after a detailed individual assessment, include six different treatments for the face, eight for the body and a further five options for the scalp and hair. From an 'Aveda Hair and Scalp Purescription Experience' to a stress-relieving 'Himalayan Rejuvenation Treatment', all nurture the body and relax the mind.

address   Strawberry Hill, Irish Town P.A., St Andrew, Jamaica

telephone   (876) 944 8400   **fax**   (876) 944 8408

room rates   from US$295

pangkor laut

This is not an adventure destination. The whole point of this emerald speck on the edge of the Straits of Malacca is that it offers nothing more – and nothing less – than shameless indulgence. And that is not as easy as it sounds.

The challenge of building exclusively for 'leisure and tranquillity' is that the emphasis on presentation is so much more acute. When guests are faced with a dawn-to-dusk itinerary, it's to be expected that certain details will go unnoticed – drop into bed exhausted and any place can look good. But doing nothing all day is only enjoyable if your surroundings are beautiful, whether they were made by man or by mother nature. For exquisite indolence magnifies the details of any environment, subjecting it to intense scrutiny.

This is nothing new; the ancient Romans invested enormous amounts of time and energy in finding appropriate locations for their Arcadian retreats, and the same again on the design and architecture. For they understood that architecture can reveal the mystery of a place; that it can embrace the complexity of a culture and landscape and distil it into something new and resonant. That is the outstanding achievement of Pangkor Laut. Its architecture has created a resort that manages to be more impressive than what was originally there. A three-hundred-acre patch of rainforest fringed by white beaches has suddenly become all the more appealing and intriguing.

In creating the design concepts for Pangkor Laut, Thai architect Lek Bunnang and American landscape architect Bill Bensley travelled extensively through Asia to draw inspiration from indigenous building methods and vernacular styles. Materials and techniques reflect tradition: the ceilings of all the villas, for example, are constructed in bamboo. The fitness centre is modelled on a mosque in Telok Intan. Some villas are set amid the dense foliage on the hillside, while others open onto the shore. But what most capture the imagination are the *kampong*-style cottages in Royal Bay and Coral Bay. These jut out over the water on stilts in the style of local wooden fishing villages. There's something intangibly exotic about living suspended above the emerald green waters of the tropics. It's as romantic as sleeping on the deck of a yacht or camping out in the desert.

Even the sarong-clad staff arrive with a touch of exotic theatre, as they parade silently along the wooden jetties with trays balanced on their shoulders. The effect is a magical impression, a lasting impression – the true distinction between the mediocre and the excellent in this business. That and of course the cuisine. As consumers we have become much more sophisticated about food, and much more demanding. We want variety as well as quality. Pangkor Laut is thoroughly in touch with what today's spoilt little travellers expect. Dining choices reflect Malaysia's international culture. Samudra, the traditional Malay restaurant, serves dishes based on coconut milk, noodles, lemongrass and spices, and is particularly good for traditional Malay desserts prepared with sago, palm sugar and coconut. Uncle Lim's Kitchen (yes, there really is an uncle Lim in the kitchen – foodies have even been known to tag along with him in the morning when he goes to market on the mainland) is an open-air restaurant perched on a rocky outcrop of Coral Bay. It specializes in Nonya Chinese cooking – local Malay cuisine prepared Chinese-style with more exotic and aromatic spices and sauces. My choice was excellent: Beggar's Chicken wrapped in lotus leaf and cooked in a salt crust.

In addition to these two restaurants, the island offers Fisherman's Cove, the Palm Grove Café, Royal Bay Beach Club, Coral Bay Pool Deck and Chapman's Bar. In sum, Pangkor Laut has seven different venues for eating – enough to satisfy the most restless epicurean.

Mr Yip, the island's resident conservationist, is on hand to take you on guided treks through the jungle and will introduce you to its numerous species, including macaque monkeys, yellow-pied hornbills, sea eagles and monitor lizards, which despite their striking resemblance to crocodiles are completely harmless. There is no local human population. Pangkor Laut is 'one island, one resort'. More than eighty per cent of it is covered by a two-million-year-old rainforest, and the proprietors intend to keep it that way. It's at the leading edge of a trend towards eco-friendly development, something in which Asia is setting the pace for the rest of the world.

address Pangkor Laut Resort, Pangkor Laut Island, 32200 Lamut, Perak, Malaysia

telephone (60) 5 699 1100 **fax** (60) 5 699 1200

room rates from RM 720

soneva fushi

The attraction of the Maldives over other island destinations is simple: more fish, less people! They offer a technicolour underwater panorama that is hard to beat, whether you are a rank amateur snorkeller or a hard-core diving enthusiast. Visiting the Maldives without diving, they say, is like walking through the Sistine Chapel without looking up.

Thirty years ago tourism scarcely existed in the Maldives. This archipelago of 1,190 islands stretching over 500 miles of the Indian Ocean southwest of Sri Lanka had just 197 visitors in 1972. The airport, a rudimentary landing strip on a stretch of coral, took the occasional Air Lanka flight from Colombo and not much more. But what the Maldives lacked in infrastructure they made up for in pure spectacle. Appearing from the air as a chain of green, white and blue amoeba-like dots, the Maldives have the most species-rich marine life in the world: 250 kinds of coral; 63 kinds of algae; and over 1,200 species of tropical fish have been recorded. The impact of man on the environment has been negligible. No wonder the water in the Maldives is said to be the clearest in the world.

Inevitably word got out about the unspoilt beauty of these islands, and they have become an irresistible magnet for travellers in search of a Robinson Crusoe-style paradise. The Republic of the Maldives now receives over 300,000 thousand visitors per annum – more than the entire native population of the islands. Yet you wouldn't know it. The Maldives' popularity is so recent that its government was able to learn from the irreparable damage caused by uncontrolled tourism elsewhere in the world. They instigated an eco-sensitive approach to tourism, based on a simple strategy: accommodate visitors only on the uninhabited islands and restrict the number of beds on each island in relation to its size. The numbers tell the story. Of the 1,190 islands, only a couple of hundred are inhabited. Two-thirds of those have a population of less than 1,000 and only four islands have more than 5,000 people. Visitors to the Maldives are distributed over 70 previously unpopulated islands. Tourism is therefore neither placing undue stress on the environment nor disrupting traditional ways of life. And travellers get what they came for – a palm-fringed island that they can (almost) call their own. There are no museums, monuments, ruins or other historical 'must sees'. There really is nothing to do but lie, guilt free, in a hammock by the beach.

That said, you should be warned: some islands fit the Robinson Crusoe fantasy better than others. The Maldives are now a popular destination for charter flights out of Germany and Switzerland and though many islands are beautiful underwater, they offer little in the way of quality architecture and design. One exception lies some 75 miles south of the capital of Malé in the Baa Atoll. Soneva Fushi on Kunfunadhoo Island goes boldly and successfully against the grain of traditional resort hotels. The bed-to-surface-area ratio is the lowest in the Maldives: 62 thatched huts of varying size and luxury accommodate a maximum of just 124 guests. Soneva Fushi offers no organized activities, no nightclub, no live entertainment and no pool. There are no cars on the island, and quite apart from an abundance of white sand beaches, green water and coral reef, it also offers what most other islands can't – a verdant jungle. The villas are all just a few feet away from their own stretch of beach and are tucked into their own private patch of jungle. Naturally canopied sand paths crisscross the island like a network of tropical boulevards, connecting its various facilities. These include a bar, a library and two restaurants located at opposite ends of a diving school. Above all the jungle gives guests complete freedom to decide just how much Robinson Crusoe-style isolation to go for.

Soneva Fushi is the personal vision of Sonu Shivdasani and his wife Eva (hence the name). Since acquiring the island just over a decade ago they have lavished their remote hundred-acre patch of white sand and dark green jungle with the sort of exacting standards and attention to minutiae that are usually reserved for private islands. All details large and small have been attended to, from the bamboo cylinders in which guests' faxes are delivered to the terracotta pots filled with water to wash the sand from your feet. The outcome, in the words of *Tatler* magazine, is 'the unspoilt and unhurried elegance of a me-me-me holiday'.

address   Soneva Fushi Resort, Kunfunadhoo, Republic of Maldives
telephone   (960) 230 304   **fax**   (960) 230 374
room rates   from US$155

las alamandas

'Tourism destroys tourism' was the perceptive comment of a Mexican minister on the blight of uncontrolled resort development. Take Puerto Vallarta, which was just a little fishing village on Mexico's Pacific coast when *Night of the Iguana* was filmed there with Ava Gardner and Richard Burton. In the late fifties and early sixties, names like Puerto Vallarta, Acapulco and Mazatlán were synonymous with paradise. Great weather, unspoilt coastline, white sandy beaches, the allure of a Latin culture … Mexico had it all. And there was no shortage of people who thought so – too many in fact. Less than four decades later these places have come to resemble the Costa Brava. They are brash resorts of high-rise hotels, package tours and fast-food franchises.

If such places exemplify what can happen if tourism is approached without planning and sensitivity, Las Alamandas shows what can happen when it is. This is probably the only stretch of Mexico's Pacific coast that still looks as it would have when the Aztecs first began making the trek here from Tenochtitlán (now Mexico City). Set on a sizeable private estate, Las Alamandas is more of a village than a resort: a collection of beautifully designed bungalows built in the style and materials of the Mexican vernacular and scattered along a stretch of private beach. There are no mariachi bands, no theme bars, no takeaway tacos … just a handful of handsome houses in lush and unspoilt surroundings.

This is not at all as it was originally planned to be. The property, a chunk of land spanning three beaches and about fifteen hundred virgin acres, was earmarked to be the next Acapulco. But the proprietor, the South American tin magnate Don Antenor Patiño, only got around to erecting a few concrete condominiums before he passed away, leaving the property to his granddaughter Isabel Goldsmith. She had very different ideas for this idyllic piece of coastline, and the next Acapulco certainly did not feature among them. Instead, she envisaged a small colony – a low-key, laid-back retreat for creative types who appreciate beautiful surroundings much more than Margaritas or mariachis.

To create Las Alamandas Goldsmith broke all the rules, and ended up with a place that appeals to people who don't like rules. This is a hotel with no set agenda … for anything. When the staff ask what you would like for dinner, they mean 'what would you like for dinner?' not 'what would you like from the menu?'

There is no menu – unless you insist on one, in which case it will be provided. Get the picture? There are no televisions or telephones in any of the guest bungalows … unless you insist, in which case there can be. You can have breakfast in the afternoon; you can ride horses on the beach, train in the secluded, air-conditioned gym, splash in the surf – whatever you want. The guiding philosophy is one of providing the guest with the rare luxury of total freedom.

That kind of freedom requires meticulous planning and rigorous attention to detail behind the scenes. The staff outnumber the guests by about fifteen to one. Why? Because someone has to be on hand when Robert De Niro wants hamburgers and beer to accompany an impromptu game of backgammon. Las Alamandas employs a small army of men just to maintain the grounds: to spray for mosquitoes at dusk, to rake the terracotta-coloured gravel paths and to tame the profusion of climbing vines, trees and native flowers that veil each carefully positioned bungalow. The endless attention to detail makes Las Alamandas very special, and as such it attracts an equally special guest list. Think of a name from the world of film, theatre or business and they've probably stayed here.

But for me the strongest feature of Las Alamandas (apart from its idyllic location) is the design. The landscaping, the architecture, the colours and the decorative detail all draw on traditions and crafts rooted deep in the national culture. The ceilings are vaulted brick, a technique common in churches and convents; walls are painted bright pink, yellow or blue – the trademark colours of both rural and contemporary Mexico; equipal chairs are ubiquitous; and *azulejos* (traditional glazed tiles) adorn the walls of the bathrooms. Every lamp, flowerpot, plate and floor tile has been sourced from some village in Mexico that has made it a speciality. Las Alamandas is, in the most complimentary sense, one of the most Mexican places in Mexico.

address Las Alamandas, PO Box 201, San Patricio Melaque, CP 48980, Mexico

telephone (52) 328 555 00   **fax** (52) 328 550 27

room rates from US$290

auberge tangaro

Painted in a simple palette of white, blue and ochre, the colours of Morocco's Atlantic coast, Auberge Tangaro is a cluster of whitewashed buildings assembled on a wind-blown point a few miles outside the town of Essaouira. Furnished simply with hand-woven rugs from the local souks and furniture made by the town's craftsmen, this former brothel was given a new lease of life by an Italian tourist who liked the area so much he decided to stay.

Being a typically style-conscious Italian, he couldn't resist doing the place up. His approach to the interiors was a combination of restraint and authenticity. Blue and white Moroccan tiles line the walls of the bathrooms and terracotta tiles cover the floors throughout. Most rooms feature little more than a bed, a table and a couple of chairs – an elegant simplicity that is most welcome in the whitewashed heat of north Africa. The very last thing you want in these sweltering temperatures is lots of fabrics and furniture. The bathrooms are spacious, with hot and cold running water and Western-style plumbing. There is no electricity, but this only adds to the charm – it means that the candlesticks in every room are more than decorative. The atmosphere, particularly at night, is reminiscent of Paul Bowles's *The Sheltering Sky*. Even the dining room is entirely illuminated by candlelight, and what it lacks in convenience is more than compensated for in romance. Auberge Tangaro is a return to the sense of oriental mystique and intrigue that has always been such a drawcard for Morocco.

With camels grazing outside the front gate and a long dusty road leading to deserted beaches, Tangaro's biggest plus is its location. Situated on the highest point of a promontory that looks back towards the town of Essaouira, it has sweeping views of the rugged wind-blown shore that makes this part of Morocco's Atlantic coast so popular with windsurfers. It is close enough to be able to dart into Essaouira for a quick coffee or an expedition to the markets, but far enough out of town to offer the beauty and seclusion of an out-of-the-way spot. Essaouira, formerly known as Mogador, was once a Portuguese trading town and is a well-known centre in Morocco for traditional crafts such as woodworking. Its appearance is so well preserved that Orson Welles chose it as a primary location for his film *Othello*. In his opinion, it resembled more closely a typical Mediterranean trading town of the seventeenth century than any other in existence.

Whitewashed and sunburned, Auberge Tangaro is typical of the style of the nearby town of Essaouira

Traditional Moroccan furniture made from the branches of the oleander tree is used throughout

Situated on a windswept promontory of the African Atlantic coast, Auberge Tangaro is a favourite with windsurfers

Fireplaces and candlesticks are not merely decorative – there is no electricity

The terrace is where breakfast and lunch are served under the shade of eucalyptus trees

Pristine and uncomplicated, the interiors are perfectly suited to the barefoot lifestyle and to the heat

This part of Morocco has its share of colourful history. Under the Romans, who took Essaouira after a tough campaign against the nomadic mountain Berbers, it became an important little trading town. A small island just off the coast was used to manufacture the rare and precious purple dye made from ground mollusc shells that denoted high rank in Roman times. So prized was this that its value was equal to that of the finest precious metals or gems.

In recent times it was more the attraction of 'purple haze' than a purple cloak that drew visitors to this sleepy fishing village. Everyone in town, not least the fast-talking stall holders in the local souks, will tell you that Jim Morrison once spent an entire summer in Essaouira – although no one seems to remember exactly where he stayed (apparently neither did he). But those were the wild sixties and times have changed some. The new tourists come for the waves, the wind and the weather (or so they say), but they still tend to stay for

weeks if not months. A lot of this has to do with the cost of living (Auberge Tangaro for example is only £30 a night including dinner and breakfast). But mainly they are seduced by the ambience. As in Bali, Byron Bay in Australia and Kerala in southern India, the lifestyle here is 'hippy-luxe'. People are laid-back and friendly, and there's a real café scene in town. The waves are ideal for surfing (when there's no wind) or windsurfing (when there's plenty, which is often).

But the best advertisement for Essaouira has to be the story of a couple I met briefly in Marrakesh. I saw them again, weeks later, at the airport and commented on how souvenir-less they were. They grinned and admitted their souvenir was too big to carry on board. It was their first time in Morocco but one week in Essaouira was enough to convince them that they had to have a house there. So they bought one, then and there, a two-storey Portuguese-style town house in the medina, the old centre, for just £14,000 sterling.

---

address Auberge Tangaro, Quartier Diabat, BP8 Essaouira, Morocco

telephone (212) 4 784 784

room rates from DH650

la gazelle d'or

The 'Golden Gazelle' is a hunting lodge deep in the south of Morocco. Located outside the old city of Taroudant, an hour inland from Agadir, La Gazelle d'Or lies in the valleys between the Atlas mountains and the sea.

It might be a hunting lodge, but it looks more like a hacienda on the plains of southern Spain than an Alpine hideaway. The entrance is reached by a very long and elegant driveway entirely screened by bamboo, a first indication of the lush oasis you are about to come upon. Surrounded by acres of green and gardens filled with towering bougainvillaea and neat rows of cypress trees, the property itself is a complex of spacious stone buildings and a collection of twenty-odd cottages. These are arranged around two huge semi-circular expanses of lawn that would look at home in the heart of Oxfordshire. Exotic clusters of oleander, jasmine, hibiscus, cactus and north African palms between the guest cottages create the impression of a verdant Eden and provide the privacy that makes this such a delightfully romantic hideaway. Outside the gates the landscape is rugged and dusty, bleached and beaten into submission by the unrelenting sun. Inside, the oasis that is La Gazelle d'Or is so luxuriously planted and

cultivated that the climate is transformed. The overbearing heat of the sun is diffused by the gardens, which provide a permanent canopy of shelter and create a refreshing breeze that gradually cools further as it travels across the numerous pools, canals and water gardens. This natural form of air-conditioning was originally discovered by the Persians, and it helps to explain how the garden came to acquire mythical status in Arabic culture – so much so that their word for heaven translates as 'garden of paradise'.

Simply walking through the gardens is a profoundly calming and soothing experience. The estate is equipped with stables, tennis courts and a large and immaculate swimming pool – yet it seems singularly ill-suited to sport. The atmosphere and ambience are more conducive to the languid pace of life of desert peoples. I'm normally not much good at doing nothing, and if anyone had suggested I'd be happy to sit and listen to two toads in a lily pond croaking at the sunset I would have laughed. But such is the seductive magic of this oasis in Morocco's deep south.

Apart from doing nothing, the day is taken up with eating. This, however, is not eating as essential nourishment but as elaborate theatre.

Sheep are La Gazelle d'Or's
organic lawnmower

Reception, where Moroccan detail
and colour are used sparingly
but effectively

Staff in traditional dress serve breakfast
on the terrace of your cottage
every morning

There is a splendid ceremony to
the preparation of traditional
thé à la menthe

The gardens are what set La Gazelle
d'Or apart – three hundred acres of
lush, perfectly manicured oasis

A detail of the wall decoration behind
the bed in each cottage

The Koran forbids the depiction of
animals or people, hence the decorative
tradition in Islamic art

The cypress and palm trees are visible
for miles in the hot and dusty
landscape of the Moroccan south

It's near enough to cycle into the
old town of Taroudant

Decoration and detailing are all genuinely Moroccan. The chair is typical of those still made in Essaouira

A Thousand and One Nights – the interior of the main building is particularly spectacular after dark

The swimming pool, set in the middle of the gardens, and the spa/massage centre

Most meals are served outside – lunch on the terrace by the pool, dinner by the main building

A traditional Berber tent is used for special functions

Colourful silks, inlaid black marble floors, brass tables and Berber portraits define the eclectically oriental interior

The hotel's mascot, a golden gazelle, recalls its origins as a hunting lodge

La Gazelle d'Or has its own stable of Arab horses for guests to ride

The Moroccans were at one time the most skilled (and feared) horsemen and riflemen in the world

Breakfast begins when you push a button on your bedside telephone to signal your readiness for the first act. In no time, a tall Moroccan in *jellaba* and *fez* arrives with a huge tray balanced on his shoulders. Croissants, pastries, traditional Moroccan pancakes and home-made marmalades are laid out on a linen tablecloth on your private terrace. It's a far cry from the buffet breakfasts of most five-star hotels.

Act two, lunch, is in a different location. Consisting of grilled fish and meat combined with a wide variety of salads grown on the property, it is served under the shade of the poolside olive trees. Bathing suits and towels are the correct attire. Dinner, the final act, is worthy of *A Thousand and One Nights*. It is served on the garden patio illuminated by candlelight from lanterns artfully arranged along the mosaic floor. Guests dress for dinner in the old-fashioned sense – dinner jackets and evening gowns – and the pace of the evening is equally dignified. Dinner lasts for hours, and the succession of courses is seemingly endless.

La Gazelle offers a taste of a Morocco that supposedly no longer exists: the Morocco of the nineteen-twenties and -thirties, when Europeans came here to live like pashas, to be intrigued by the mysterious and exotic culture, and to marvel at the extraordinary gardens such a hot and dry country could produce.

If you cannot stomach quite so much indulgence, then a simple remedy is to hire a four-wheel drive and explore the surrounding area. This is the untamed south, a rugged landscape of spectacular canyons, palm-tree-filled gorges and idyllic, time-forgotten villages. But what about the hunting? This is, after all, a very popular destination for shooting holidays. Some even travel with their own loaders. They leave before daybreak and, with the help of beaters, shoot turtledoves (a plague according to locals, because they steal all the wheat). Some enthusiasts have been coming here for almost two decades, though personally I can't fathom how shooting can possibly compete with the pure indulgence of doing nothing.

address La Gazelle d'Or, BP 260, Taroudant, Morocco

telephone (212) 885 2039 **fax** (212) 885 2737

room rates from DH4580

les deux tours

In the postwar Moroccan setting of Paul Bowles's classic novel *The Sheltering Sky*, hotels like Les Deux Tours didn't exist. His protagonists, American travellers Port and Kit Moresby, were faced with two choices: grand luxury or fleapit. The small luxurious retreat was not yet on the menu.

They would certainly have stayed at Les Deux Tours had they had the chance. It gets its name from the two mud towers that define the impressive entrance. Massive wooden doors, the kind so distinctive of the Moorish style, lead to a series of small courtyards overgrown with lush bougainvillaea. Another set of arched doorways open to a magnificently tiled interior which in turn leads into a larger internal courtyard and garden complete with an exquisite swimming pool. This is everything you long for Marrakesh to be – exotic, colourful and mysterious. Every room faces a courtyard or hidden patio and the bathrooms are like nothing I have ever seen elsewhere: baroque towers in mud bricks decorated with the most fanciful architectural features. Deep sunken baths built into alcoves, towering domed ceilings, ornate mosaic tiling combined with traditional *tadlekt* finishes: this is the very embodiment of the oriental fantasy.

Les Deux Tours is a complex of villas set in an exotic walled garden. Inside the gates is a fragrant and multi-coloured explosion of jasmine, oleander and bougainvillaea; outside is the exact opposite, a vast expanse of hostile sunburned desert punctuated with great regularity by clumps of date palms. It is an oasis straight out of Lawrence of Arabia, yet it is still in the city, an area of Marrakesh known as the Palmeraie.

The Palmeraie is the stuff of legend, a centuries-old sickle-shaped expanse of palm trees surrounding the city on three sides that has been marvelled at by many an adventurer. Until relatively recently it was strictly off-limits for building of any kind. Today, some construction is allowed provided no palm trees are damaged and that a house or group of houses stand in a minimum of two hectares of open space. This surprisingly rigorous conservation code has ensured that the Palmeraie has preserved its enchanting appearance and confirmed it as the most desirable location in Marrakesh.

The medina, the old walled city dating back to the twelfth century, is only fifteen minutes' drive away, but the sheer contrast makes it feel much further. Its labyrinthine passageways, filled with all the smells, sounds and sights of a medieval metropolis, are the very antithesis of the desert-like tranquillity and sparseness of the Palmeraie. That's what makes Les Deux Tours the perfect location from which to experience Marrakesh. When the heat and the hustle-bustle of the souks gets too much, you can retreat to the soothing pace of life in the palm grove.

Les Deux Tours was the brainchild of Marrakesh-based architect Charles Boccara. Born in Tunisia, educated in Paris, Boccara has made his name with an architecture that borrows from the history and culture of southern Morocco. Like the tantalizingly beautiful and exotic *ksour* – Berber fortresses situated in the verdant gorges on the edge of the Sahara – his buildings are in mud. They make use in a modern fashion of building techniques and materials that are indigenous to Morocco's south. Boccara himself fights a continuous battle (along with a handful of other Marrakesh-based architects such as

Elie Mouyal) against the onslaught of the nondescript concrete bunker, which threatens to wipe out a building tradition dating back more than a thousand years.

Thus it is not entirely fanciful to say that Les Deux Tours feels and looks as Marrakesh ought to; that was precisely the intention. The materials (wood, mud bricks, mosaic tiles), the forms (dome-topped towers, crenellated walls, hidden courtyards), and the colours (pink, purple, yellow, red, blue and black) are all ingredients of Morocco's fascinating history and are interpreted and applied in a thoroughly modern manner. Even the decorative details throughout the compound – the rugs, carpets, plates, bowls, vases, lanterns and tables – are all the work of Moroccan craftsmen.

Les Deux Tours evokes the mystique, the exoticism and the vibrancy of Morocco's culture, yet without nostalgia. There is no better introduction to one of north Africa's most fascinating cities.

address Les Deux Tours, BP 513 Marrakesh-Principal, Douar Abiad Circuit de la Palmeraie de Marrakesh, Morocco
telephone (212) 4329 525 **fax** (212) 4329 523
room rates from DH1250

amanwana

Just getting to Amanwana is an adventure. The easy bit is flying to Bali's Denpasar airport. Thereafter the planes keep getting smaller and the temperature hotter. First there's a local flight to Lombok, followed by a hop over a spectacular volcano to Sumbawa airport (which looks less like an airport than an abandoned garage with a very long driveway). Then it's a quick jog across the island of Sumbawa in a minivan to a marina of sorts where a sport fishing boat takes you for the final hour-long crossing of a turquoise blue bay to Moyo Island.

By Indonesian standards Moyo is virtually deserted. A few thousand people live in a clutch of villages on one side of the island, and that is it. The rest is wild and it offers plenty of adventure. Ours started almost immediately because the jetty where guests normally disembark had been blown away in the last typhoon, leaving no alternative but the service jetty at the other end of the bay. Off the boat it was straight into a convoy of camouflage-green open jeeps for a ten-minute rumble through the jungle to reach our tents.

'Tent' in this case turns out to be about as appropriate as calling Versailles a house. This is camping out maharaja-style. Every tent comes complete with living room, writing desk, ample closets, double wash basins, shower with hot and cold running water and a separately enclosed toilet. A tent with a bathroom? Even Shah Jahan, builder of the Taj Mahal, could not boast such luxuries in the palatial tent he took with him on his extended hunting trips. It's almost embarrassing to admit that they are air-conditioned to boot. But if at first this seems to be pandering too much to fragile urbanites, after a day of adventure in the steamy equatorial climate of Moyo Island the cool relief of a sound night's sleep quickly dispels any guilt you may feel at not roughing it 'properly'. You might well ask why they did not just build cottages or houses. The answer is that tents, no matter how sumptuous, remain more in keeping with the spirit of the island. This is a nature reserve, a slice of pristine tropical jungle, and tents maintain at least the illusion that your intrusion on paradise is only temporary and of little consequence.

Mother nature is the star here and she has more than a few surprises in store for the fortunate few who come to camp in one of her most spectacular backyards. Rise early and you may witness entire families of monkeys: the parents foraging for food and the youngsters using any unoccupied tents as trampolines.

Camping out maharaja-style.
Amanwana's are the way tents should be
– simple, spacious and comfortable

Low tide reveals a coral reef no more
than a yard from the shore

The odd sculptural touch only adds to
Amanwana's sophisticated blend of
pure nature and indulgent luxury

A spa pool shows the extent to which the
design acknowledges the surroundings

Each tent has a dressing area
and bathroom

An entire fleet of boats is available to
guests. The slower, more traditional
ones are the more popular

Moyo Island is only accessible by boat
from the island of Sumbawa, an hour
and a half away

A thatched pavilion in the traditional
Indonesian style serves as dining
room and bar

Although a nature reserve hardly needs
to be landscaped, it is complemented by
odd touches such as these old ceramics

Staff outnumber the guests at Amanwana by at least three to one

Moyo Island is a protected nature reserve and is virtually uninhabited

The jungle throws a verdant cloak over everything and makes the temperatures bearable

A sitting room in a tent is not as redundant as it seems – it's a welcome air-conditioned retreat from the heat

All tents at Amanwana are identical. The only difference is location: edge of beach or edge of jungle

Mosquito nets are a must here; air-conditioning is an individual option

Shaded by towering trees, the tents are largely camouflaged by their surroundings

At the far end of the bay a wooden platform is all that remains of the jetty washed away by a recent cyclone

The island is famed for its exotic sunsets, particularly in the rainy season

In the dry season deer make their way into camp to graze on the grass. The bay, just outside the front door of the tent, is a thin emerald veil concealing an impossibly colourful coral reef teeming with countless schools of tropical fish (the kind that glossy airline magazines are so fond of). For some of the most sensational snorkelling in the world you need do no more than wade in from the beach and stick your head in the water. Further out in the lagoon a family of sea turtles rarely moves more than a couple of hundred yards in either direction, and for the serious scuba-diver a dramatic sea wall awaits a few hundred yards from the beach, where the reef descends like an underwater cliff into a darker and even more exotic world of sharks, giant octopuses and streamlined manta rays.

Everything at Amanwana is there to help you explore and discover. There is a diving school complete with facilities for lessons in underwater photography. A fleet of nineteen boats caters to every possible water-based whim, including sailing and deep sea sport fishing, and there is a well-stocked garage of open-top four-wheel drives that can transport you to the remotest corners of the island.

Taking in Moyo's natural spectacle is a full-time activity and consequently the atmosphere at night is low key. Breakfast, lunch and dinner are served in a traditional Indonesian thatched pavilion. The food is good and the service impeccable, but most guests are too tired to notice. This is not a party-till-you-drop place; everyone is in their tent by ten.

With 135 staff on hand to make sure you want for nothing, and a maximum of 40 guests at any one time, every whim can be catered to: breakfast in your own tent, dinner on the beach by candlelight and a bonfire; there is even a massage centre on the edge of the jungle in a remote part of the lagoon. The consistent theme is of luxury and simplicity combined with breathtaking natural beauty. All of the benefits and none of the drawbacks – now that's a real escape.

---

address Amanwana, Moyo Island, West Sumbawa Regency, Indonesia

telephone (62) 371 22233 **fax** (62) 371 22288

room rates from US$590

cotton house

Like most islands in the Caribbean, Mustique in the Grenadines was once a sugar plantation. In the seventeenth and eighteenth centuries sugar was the new commodity and its cultivation could yield vast profits. For the colonial powers, the Caribbean was well suited to growing sugar cane because there was plenty of land and sun, not to mention an indigenous population, the Caribs, whom they could conveniently enslave on the grounds that they were cannibals. When the native population was exhausted, boatloads of slaves were brought from Africa to continue the backbreaking work. But in time, with the shift of large-scale sugar cane cultivation to Asia, the West Indies became less competitive and the plantations, including that of Mustique, were abandoned. Today its restored remains, including the windmill and warehouse, form the core of the Cotton House hotel.

So why, you may ask, is it called the Cotton House? The story behind the name is, in a sense, the story of modern Mustique. This three-square-mile island just south of St Vincent was by the fifties just an abandoned bit of sunburned scrub inhabited by the odd fisherman and his family. And so it might have remained if a young Colin Tennant, a.k.a. Lord Glenconner, had not adopted it. The scion of a wealthy aristocratic family from Scotland, he had set out for the West Indies to inspect long-forgotten family holdings. While in St Lucia, he heard about an island that was for sale and immediately took the first mail boat out to see it. Despite its craggy, unkempt appearance his imagination was fired and he promptly cabled his father to advise him of his plan to buy. His father replied that he was 'in full accordance providing there is water'. There wasn't, but that didn't stop the young lord from paying £45,000 sterling (a small fortune in 1959) for an island without buildings, services or water.

Fuelled by enthusiasm Tennant set about making the island habitable. His first grand plan was to convert the ruins of the sugar plantation into a working cotton plantation. Against great odds (and at enormous expense) he managed to bring in a crop, but only one: he was forced to stop when his accountants calculated that every shirt woven from his fine cotton had cost £3,000.

Undaunted, Tennant turned his manic drive and extravagant imagination to a more sybaritic goal – that of turning Mustique into an earthly paradise for family and friends. In those days nobody had heard of Mustique.

The Great House, now the living/dining room and bar, was the old sugar plantation's warehouse

Shabby chic in the Caribbean: Indian silk, white cotton slip covers and dark wood colonial chairs

Guests are accommodated in a collection of small cottages spread around the estate

In true colonial fashion, dinner is served on the veranda of the Great House

Theatre set designer Oliver Messel was responsible for the design of the pool house, known as Messel's Folly

A fondness for French doors with oval fanlights is a typical design signature of Messel's work

The Cotton House estate is the prime location on Mustique, located between L'Ansecoy Bay and Endeavor Bay

Colonial eclecticism extends to the smallest details, including this velvet cushion depicting an exotic scene

The diving school specializes in classes for absolute beginners

Coutinot House has a wraparound terrace that overlooks Endeavor Bay

Beyond the mill, on a point overlooking the rugged Atlantic coast of L'Ansecoy Bay, is Baliceau Cottage with four suites

Beach baroque – a shell-encrusted cupboard in the Great House is typical of Messel's eccentric excess

The Cotton House diving school on Endeavor Bay is a typical Caribbean shed on the beach

The Monkey Bar in the Great House has been Mustique's main place of mischief for over two decades

From the balcony of Coutinot House, the view takes in the quiet Caribbean (as opposed to Atlantic surfing beaches)

The Cotton House is furnished in classic colonial style with linens, cottons, rattan furniture and polished wooden floors

The stone windmill, workhorse of the original sugar plantation, is still a landmark on the property

Without being too formal, the ambience of the Great Room has a sense of elegant heritage

Awareness of the island was given a boost when Tennant gave Princess Margaret (a distant relative) a parcel of land as a wedding present. There were no roads to speak of at that time, nor even electricity until 1972. Yet the newly formed Mustique Company pressed ahead with creating a hotel to house guests invited to the island to consider buying land.

The imposing storage house with its foot-thick stone walls and typical veranda became the dining room, the ballroom, and the popular Monkey Bar. In true colonial style, the 'rough and ready' was set aside at night, when guests would dress for dinner and be entertained by some sort of show that the irrepressible Tennant had managed to conjure. Attracted by Mustique's promise of privacy, ideal weather and perfect beaches, as well as the advantage of being out of the hurricane zone, many big names signed on the dotted line. Mick Jagger, David Bowie and Tommy Hilfiger are among those who were approved (while the Aga Khan and the Shah of Iran were apparently rejected).

Cotton House is a collection of houses dotted around a lush estate, each with a view, and guests are accommodated in a house of their own. It has the best location on this man-made Eden, on a promontory that divides windswept L'Ansecoy Bay from the calm green waters the other side. Surfing and snorkelling are therefore both just a stone's throw away.

Despite the stories of wild times and crazy parties, Mustique's present-day appearance – immaculate and unspoilt – is the result of rigorous efforts. No helicopters are allowed on the island and the landing strip accommodates nothing bigger than a six-seater. The airport, like the nearby church, was built in bamboo, and there is no traffic to speak of – everyone gets around on a Mule. This is not quite as rustic as it sounds: Mule is the brand name of Kawasaki's motorized golf carts. These only have two gears (forward and back) but there are still speed bumps all over the island – noise is micro-managed like everything else here. Paradise, it seems, takes relentless planning.

address Cotton House, PO Box 349, Mustique, St Vincent, West Indies

telephone (1) 784 456 4777 **fax** (1) 784 456 5887

room rates from US$590

pousada de nossa senhora da assunção

The convents of Portugal are as characteristic a feature of its countryside as the chateaux of France. Yet not all are as they used to be. Many suffered badly in the course of the nineteenth century, when the Church lost first its influence and then its land. Quite a few prime properties passed into private hands to be converted into country houses. These were the lucky ones. Many simply fell to ruin and neglect. Had it not been for a creative scheme developed in recent years by the government they might have disappeared altogether.

The Pousadas of Portugal is a national hotel project charged with restoring historical architecture, preserving regional values and enriching tourism with a sense of cultural integrity. Anyone who doubts that governments are able to do such things in a convincing and stylish manner should see the Pousada de Nossa Senhora da Assunção. Situated in a valley below the old city of Arraiolos in the sunbaked plains of Alentejo, seventy-five miles outside Lisbon, this imposing former convent had its beginnings as a private estate. In the absence of hereditary descendants, it was bequeathed to the order of St John the Evangelist, otherwise known as the Blue Canons because of the colour of their habits.

The monastery here was founded in 1527 in celebration of the day of the Assumption of our Blessed Lady. Built in a mixture of the Portuguese Manueline and Renaissance styles, it remained a monastery until the general abolition of religious orders in 1834, when it was returned to private hands. The Arraiolan family of Mexia Lobo Côrte-Real converted the monastery for use as a holiday home, which is how it stayed until 1983, when their descendants sold it to the state. By then it still had historical significance, but little else; the place was a wreck.

It is much to the credit of the Portuguese government that they chose architect José Paulo dos Santos to rescue it. Dos Santos defined his approach to this sensitive task in the phrase 'step forward and be silent'. The resulting Pousada is a place to be noticed while remaining true to the serene spirit of the cloister. Its elegant, meditative minimalism represents the kind of design statement that wouldn't be out of place in the hippest hotels of New York, Paris or London, and yet here, in the heart of the Portuguese countryside, it seems even more appropriate. The materials chosen for the renovation – granite, limestone and plaster – are those of the original structure.

Even the furniture in the guest rooms evokes the centuries-old monastic tradition of functional simplicity. Enormous terracotta pots punctuating the interior spaces and the outdoor courtyards recall the agricultural wealth of the Alentejan plains, and many of the stucco ceilings, carved relief panels and restored arcades are painted in the blue of the Canons. Even the surrounding land is once again given over to pasture for grazing horses and to olive groves for the production and bottling of oil.

Dos Santos's thoroughly modern, pared-down approach reinforces both the spiritual and the spatial qualities of the former monastery. Yet don't assume that because Pousada de Nossa Senhora retains its atmosphere of serenity it is a solemn place to stay. Only the peace is monastic. There is nothing austere in the experience of being a guest here. Among the labyrinthine vaulted spaces are two separate restaurants and a bar. The food is excellent – surprisingly so for a state-run affair. A typical menu might include soft cheese with penny royal sauce followed by grilled dam fish with herbs. There is also a series of courtyards used for outdoor dining in the summer months, and the swimming pool, a vast stone-edged basin, is set on a purpose-built terrace that overlooks the surrounding farmland. Rooms are spacious and beautifully appointed with wooden floors, marble-panelled bathrooms and modern furniture with linen slip covers. There is nothing in the view to detract from the harmonious atmosphere. You cannot catch so much as a glimpse of highways, electricity pylons or other twentieth-century eyesores – only acres and acres of olive trees and verdant oaks marching up and down the rolling hills.

Pousada de Nossa Senhora da Assunção should be a role model for restoration projects. It is proof not only that the modern and the antique make a potent combination, but that even governments can make funky hosts when steered in the right direction.

---

address Pousada de Nossa Senhora da Assunção, 7040 Arraiolos, Portugal

telephone (351) 66 41 9 340   **fax** (351) 66 41 9 280

room rates from Esc 20,300

singita

Contemporary design, a modern health spa, indulgent cuisine and a wine cellar with twelve thousand vintage bottles: these are things not normally associated with a safari expedition. But at Singita they are exactly what you get. This is an African experience for people who have no interest in sacrificing creature comforts for the sake of adventure.

Located on the edge of the world-famous Kruger National Park in the Sabi Sand Reserve, Singita is a seventy-five-minute flight by charter plane from Johannesburg. This is not your ordinary connecting flight. It's more than likely that you will fly over herds of buffalo and elephants along the way and the pilot is quite likely to apologize for a violent swerve because he had to avoid a vulture. The safari that started in the plane continues with the drive from the airstrip to Singita Game Reserve. During the day impala, zebra and water buffalo are the most likely large game to be seen; the lions and leopards prefer to hunt at night or in the cool of dusk.

Singita is split into two separate lodges, each situated on the banks of the Sand River, half a mile or so apart. Ebony Lodge is designed in a turn-of-the-century, leather wing-chair colonial style, while Boulders Lodge is more contemporary. In both, the accommodation is an elaborate 'all suite' affair. Boulders features nine guest houses (air-conditioned, of course) each with their own living area, double-sided fireplace (with a sort of witch's hat steel grate that swivels to direct the heat to either the living room or the bedroom) and private swimming pool. The common area is a lofty, open-plan space with gleaming, dark polished-concrete floors, massive easy chairs with crisp white linen dust covers and oversize throw pillows covered in traditional African cloth. For want of a more precise term, I would call the style 'organic Africa-graphica' – but however you describe it, 'roughing it' in dusty khakis this is not.

It's a hell of a way to be introduced to South Africa's veld. This place is so indulgently luxurious, so comfortable, so accommodating that it stimulates you to want to do precisely nothing. And therein lies the only problem you're likely to run into at Singita – torn between the call of the wild and the debilitating desire for a nap, what's a hedonist to do? It's a miracle that guests can be lured from their sumptuous huts at all (though be assured that Singita does mean 'the miracle' in the local Shangaan language).

Singita is billed as Africa's finest private game reserve, and not only because of its refined sense of hospitality. Extending over 50,000 acres of the Sabi Sand ecosystem, it is in the very heartland of Africa and is home to giraffes, lions, leopards, elephants, rhinos and zebras (to name just a few of its species). All of them can be tracked for shooting (with a camera) on foot or in an open vehicle in the company of a professional ranger and a skilled Shangaan tracker. Landrover excursions are limited to six passengers and a network of radio contact helps alert your ranger to the whereabouts of game. It is all set up to maximize your chances of seeing Africa's unique and exotic wildlife – up close. How up close? Well be prepared for the shout 'there's a hippo on the lawn', because at dusk they're often found feeding in the grounds. The personal game guard assigned to escort guests from their suite to dinner in the open-air reed *boma* (the palisaded dining area) is perhaps not so redundant after all.

But with private swimming pools, elaborate meals, outdoor massages on your own teak deck overlooking the bush … when is there time for a real safari? Chances are you will be roused on your first morning at what would normally be considered an ungodly hour. But don't even think about diving back into bed. It's thoroughly worth it. Dawn and dusk are when the veld comes alive and not only might you witness a giraffe giving birth, lions mating or an elephant devouring an entire tree, you'll be able to reflect on your first expedition over a bush breakfast of champagne, eggs scrambled over a wood fire, smoked leg of impala, eland sausages, strawberries and fresh honeycomb.

I don't care how long you've subscribed to *National Geographic* or how many wildlife documentaries you've seen – nothing, absolutely nothing can hold a candle to the adrenalin rush of experiencing the African wilderness at first hand. And luckily for Singita, no amount of luxury and pampering can deflate the thrill.

---

address Singita Private Game Reserve, Ground Floor, PGBI House, 53 Autumn Road, Rivonia, Sandton 2128, South Africa

telephone (27) 11 234 0990   **fax** (27) 11 234 0535

room rates from R 3400

casa de carmona

Carmona is one of the most important historic towns in Spain. Its civilization can be traced back five thousand years and over the ages it has been ruled by the Phoenicians, the Carthaginians and the Romans, among others. One of its surviving city gates ranks among the finest ancient Roman portals to be found anywhere in the former empire. But Carmona's greatest period was the eight hundred years of Moorish rule in the south of Spain. Moorish El Andalus included the cities of Seville, Cordoba and Granada, and the distinctive Arabic culture of this part of southern Spain was the most enlightened of all the regions conquered by the followers of Mohammed. While most of Europe was still floundering in the Dark Ages, Moorish Spain was spectacularly successful in science, architecture and the arts. Mathematics, music and highly skilled handcraft thrived under the enlightened and tolerant rule of southern Spain's Caids. The Moors were also great potters and ceramists and their colourful tiles played a big role in defining Moorish architecture. Since the depiction of living things was forbidden by the Koran, geometry became their art. Intricate compositions in small mosaic tiles decorated the walls and floors of already ornate buildings.

This golden age of Arabic culture wasn't to last. After centuries of warfare against the 'infidel' Moors, the Castilian north, under Queen Isabella and King Ferdinand, finally drove them out of Spain in 1492. Yet a glimpse of the splendour of El Andalus can still be found in a renovated Moorish palace in the heart of Carmona, now little more than a sleepy whitewashed village. When Doña Marta Medina, an aristocrat, art historian and architect from one of Seville's oldest families, first bought the dilapidated sixteenth-century palace in the late eighties she had no plans to make it a hotel. She wanted only to create a magnificent apartment for herself and to leave the rest in 'splendid ruin'. But the World Expo '92 in Seville changed all that. Inspired by the international attention the fair would draw to the area she decided instead to take on the mammoth task of renovating the entire building to create a small luxury hotel.

To hear Doña Marta tell it, building a new palace from scratch would have been easier. Walls of monumental stone blocks do not readily lend themselves to the installation of modern essentials such as smoke detectors, automatic sprinklers and ducted air-conditioning, not to mention thirty bathrooms.

A detail of the studded front gate
of Casa de Carmona in Andalusia

The pool, in keeping with Moorish
tradition, is tucked into a
courtyard of its own

Unmistakably Spanish, the massive
front gates set the theme

The front courtyard would originally
have been used for turning
coaches around

The sheer scale of the staircase reveals
the architectural pedigree of what was
once a Moorish nobleman's palace

The vaulted spaces of the poolside
conservatory

Long, tall and narrow, the formal rooms
(this is the Music Room) are arranged
around the main courtyard

Ochre and terracotta: the colours of the
ancient Romans and the Moors alike

Casa de Carmona is located in the centr
of Carmona, one of the oldest towns
in southern Spain

The grand apartment is one of the rooms available to guests. It's also used as a conference room

The impressive staircase leads from the main courtyard to the first-floor balcony level

The exterior of the poolside conservatory where breakfast is served in the summer

Enormous decorative terracotta pots are a reminder of the wealth the area once derived from olive plantations

A classical statue at reception recalls Carmona's status as one of Spain's key Roman cities

The library, a dark and soothing space where pre-dinner drinks are served

Interior architect Doña Marta Medina imported all the bath fittings and taps from England

Another corner of the library, this one overlooking the pool courtyard beyond

Leading from the entrance gate is the first of a series of courtyards

Despite countless setbacks and bureaucratic tangles, the entire project was completed in eighteen months, just in time for the Seville Expo of 1992.

Casa de Carmona is nothing less than a small palace. That's the best, indeed the only way to describe it. The paintings, the furniture, even the smallest decorative details are all of a quality and beauty that belong to a wealthy ancestral home. With every room, including all thirty-odd guest rooms, crowded with art and antiques, it's easy to imagine the Andalusian nobility residing here. The courtyards and gardens, the hidden spaces, the tall narrow rooms, the typical mosaic tile decoration, and the bold terracotta red of the walls all conspire to make this a place of considerable aesthetic impact. Set against the powerful Moorish architecture it becomes an irresistible experience – a chance to live amid the authentic style and opulence of one of the world's great cultures. And that was exactly the intention.

Doña Marta Medina is passionate about El Andalus and she laments the lack of scholarly attention devoted to the beautiful buildings, large and small, that the Moors left behind. Here she has made a practical effort to redress the balance, in the process creating a magical, intoxicating place to stay – so magical that it's tempting never to leave the confines of the house. With a pool, a courtyard garden, a library and of course a restaurant serving delicious Andalusian specialities such as gazpacho, you never need be bored or go hungry … though you might very well miss the benefits of Carmona's extraordinary location. Seville, a heady mix of old and new, is only twenty miles away; Cordoba, with its famous Mezquita mosque, is only an hour's journey, as is the national park of Doñana with its unspoilt beaches and spectacular wildlife sanctuary. Thus Casa de Carmona is a handy place from which to explore Andalusia. But it's also a great place to hang around and do nothing – in great style.

---

address Casa de Carmona, Plaza de Lasso 1, 41410 Seville, Spain

telephone (34) 5 419 1000 **fax** (34) 5 419 0189

room rates from Ptas 18,000

hacienda benazuza

Since the tenth century, the hacienda of Benazuza has been one of the most important estates in southern Spain. Founded in the time of the Moors, who planted 15,000 olive and fig trees on 5,000 acres of land overlooking the fertile plain of Seville, the continued prosperity of Benazuza was ensured by Ferdinand II. Ferdinand – canonized as Fernando el Santo – successfully reconquered Córdoba and Seville from the Moors and then was astute enough to seek their expert advice on matters of farming.

Even the term hacienda has its origins in Moorish times, when the architecture of the farm was dictated by what was being cultivated. Properties with olive groves were distinguished by a tower (allowing the proprietor to climb above the trees to observe the estate) whereas *cortijos*, farms for cereal crops, were lower and flatter. The haciendas of Seville have thus survived as a fascinating and very particular form of rural architecture. Some supported substantial populations and were extraordinary examples of industry and productivity.

When Ferdinand's son Alfonso X inherited the property he returned to Aragon, leaving Benazuza to the crusading order of the Knights of Santiago. It remained a monastery until the sixteenth century, when Charles I of Spain,

hungry for funds to finance his campaigns against Italy and Turkey, reappropriated it and sold it to the Duke of Béjar in 1539, who, in turn, leased it to Francisco Duarte, purveyor of the imperial armies and navies. The Duarte family stayed for three centuries, and it was during their tenure that Felipe IV granted the title of Count of Benazuza to the head of the estate. Ironically, the name Benazuza was that of the long line of Saracen princes who dwelled here for seven centuries prior to the Christian conquest.

So large had the workforce of Benazuza become by this time that civil and criminal law were administered from its salon by permission of the king. Only in the nineteenth century, with the industrial revolution and the spread of mechanization, did the prosperity that had sustained these communities for many centuries as virtually independent civic powers begin to be eroded. Many haciendas were abandoned, and only those able to reinvent themselves survived. Benazuza was lucky: it was sold to the Pablo Romero family, famous for breeding Spain's best fighting bulls.

Today, Benazuza has entered a new phase of its long, eventful history. It is now a five-star hotel just twenty minutes' drive from Seville.

Hacienda Benazuza was a prosperous olive estate – a fact brought home by the size of the property's chapel

Like the architecture of the Andalusian *finca* or farmhouse, furniture is plain, sturdy and distinctly masculine

Whitewashed walls and the odd patch of red or ochre are deeply characteristic of the south of Spain

The old warehouse where the oil was pressed is now the hotel's reception area and guests' lounge

The Moorish style is still evident in Andalusian buildings – even, ironically, in Christian churches of the region

Oak beams, red upholstery and the rugged texture of roughly plastered walls typify the style of El Andalus

Its history gives an idea of the grandeur of the architecture and design, but to their credit the new owners resisted the temptation to smother the former farmhouse with luxury. The church has been carefully restored (it is used today for weddings and other occasions), the stables are almost untouched, and the courtyard and pathways were repaved in a rugged manner that suits the heritage of the property. Rather than disguise its long life as an olive plantation, the tools of the hacienda's former industry have been used as decoration. The mills, pots and vats used for pressing and storing olive oil are arranged like sculpture throughout the public spaces. The massive stone pressing wheel, the copper cylinders for taking oil to market, the weighing mechanism (for olive oil was historically sold by weight) and the enormous terracotta pots buried up to their rims in the ground to catch the oil from the pressing wheel are artfully arranged around chairs and in conversation corners. Thankfully there isn't an explanatory plaque in sight.

Haciendas were never meant to be glamorously furnished. That was what city palaces were for. Out here in the *campo*, utility and simplicity were of the essence. Terracotta paved floors, whitewashed walls with the odd splash of ochre and sturdy furniture in dark-stained solid wood are the decorative hallmarks of a typical Andalusian hacienda. The luxury is in the space, the serenity, the shade and coolness, and in the pleasure garden, another Arabic hand-me-down to Spanish culture.

A telling sign of the success of Hacienda Benazuza's makeover is that many of the guests are Spanish. The food probably has a lot to do with it. Like the architecture, it is simple but refined. As well as Andalusian specialities there is always a seasonal menu (it featured game during my stay). The Benazuza kitchen has gained quite a reputation, and many residents of Seville will journey out into the country to experience its fare. So if you find the restaurant empty at ten at night, that is just because its mostly Spanish diners haven't arrived yet.

address Hacienda Benazuza, 41800 Sanlúcar la Mayor, Seville, Spain

telephone (34) 95 570 33 44   **fax** (34) 95 570 34 10

room rates from Ptas 39,000

the ice hotel

'The world's largest igloo' is how the brochure describes it, and technically this is correct. A fairy tale structure in the wintry landscape north of Sweden's Arctic Circle, the Ice Hotel is a fascinating example of a building in snow and ice. But this is no Eskimo hut – it's a palace, a castle cut from frozen crystal.

Consider the statistics: the Ice Hotel covers 40,000 square feet and accommodates over a hundred guests. It has an ice bar, an indoor curling lane, an ice cinema (specializing in films about northern adventure), a viewing platform (to catch the aurora borealis if you're lucky), a sculpture garden and an ice gallery, not to mention an ice chapel that is very popular for baptisms and weddings. All this takes about 30,000 tons of snow and 5,000 tons of ice to realize every winter ... because, come May, the whole place simply melts away.

The ice used in constructing the Ice Hotel has little in common with your everyday ice cube. The pillars, bed frames, church pews, cinema seats, windows and even the fibre-optic-lit chandeliers are all cut from the ice of the adjacent River Torne. The ice of a flowing river is under constant pressure as it forms, giving it a structural strength that makes it suitable for use as a building material.

But even if its design is far more elaborate, the Ice Hotel still functions as an igloo. The science of an igloo is based on the fact that the best protection from a snow storm is, ironically, a shelter made out of snow. As Arne Bergh, creator of the Ice Hotel, will tell you, snow is a great insulator (against light and cold), and yet it also breathes. So the inside temperature of the hotel remains a constant minus 4–7° Celsius whether outside temperatures reach record lows of minus 40° or a positively balmy plus 5°.

Even so, why would anyone of sound mind and body travel to a place where the indoor temperature is 5° below zero? That's easy – because on this entire planet there is nothing, absolutely nothing like it. The beauty of the place is spellbinding. The colour of the ice changes according to the weather and the time of day – it can be green, blue, grey or turquoise, and the entire structure melts back into the river each spring. Even a cynic must admire the pure poetry of such a cycle.

Being spellbound by its beauty is one thing, but what's it like to stay here? That's the question most people ask. Surprisingly, this monument in snow and ice is more congenial than its average temperatures might indicate.

The Swedes are completely unperturbed by below-zero thermometer readings – for them it's simply a matter of 'appropriate' or 'inappropriate' clothing. It's true that standing in the Absolut Ice Bar nursing a hollowed-out block of ice filled with vodka is perfectly comfortable so long as you're wearing a cosy snowsuit. (The snow suits, boots and gloves are supplied by the hotel's ever-helpful 'igloo guides'.) Sure everyone looks like a teddy bear – but then blue skin is not too attractive either.

Beds are wooden platforms suspended on massive blocks of ice with a foam mattress covered by a thick layer of overlapping reindeer skins. Arctic sleeping bags make it possible to sleep in a room the temperature of a meat-packing plant. Dozens of candles are tucked into ice nooks and crannies throughout the room. It might look rather romantic but any ideas of *amour* are cut dead by the fact that the sleeping bags are like quilted coffins, strictly for one person only. Besides, the effort of extinguishing all the candles and manoeuvring yourself (fully clothed) into the bag is exhausting. But you can forget worrying about having to get up in the middle of the night: once you're out … you're out cold!

The next thing you register is the cup of hot berry juice brought to your bedside in the morning by a smiling igloo guide. So now to the second most asked question: what is there to do? Lots! This is Swedish Lapland, a never-ending white wilderness that is home to the indigenous Sami people. It is a perfect playground for snowmobile safaris, cross-country skiing, downhill skiing, ice fishing and dog sledding. Winter lasts from November to April, and activities and facilities are all superbly organized (in typical Scandinavian fashion). The Ice Hotel maintains an entire fleet of shiny snowmobiles, not to mention an arsenal of clothing and accessories. Lapland is a popular destination, and there are regular flights from Stockholm. Swedes, it seems, need a fix of ice and snow in the way we need a regular dose of beach and sun.

---

address The Ice Hotel, Marknadsvägen 63, S-981 91 Jukkasjärvi, Sweden

telephone (46) 980 668 00 **fax** (46) 980 668 90

room rates from SEK 850

ngorongoro crater lodge

'It was Africa distilled up through six thousand feet like the strong and refined essence of a continent ... The views were immensely wide – everything that you saw made for greatness and freedom and unequalled nobility.' Karen Blixen's haunting reference to Tanzania's Ngorongoro Crater in *Out of Africa* is an appropriate introduction to what is, surely, Africa's masterpiece.

Nearly three million years old, the ancient remains of this once active volcano shelter one of the most beautiful wildlife havens left on earth. The rare black rhino is still to be found within its rainforest-encrusted rim, giant-tusked elephants still wander the forests climbing the crater's great slopes, black-maned lions stalk the grasslands, and pink flamingos still crowd the soda lakes scattered along the crater's twelve-mile width. But above all, this monument to nature – the 'Baroness of Africa' – stirs our deepest emotions because it is the centre of the planet. It is the place where man stood up and walked for the first time. This key moment in our common ancestry is somehow symbolized by the beauty and nobility of the Masai warrior, tall, proud and majestic, and clothed as colourfully as the landscape that he calls home.

Ngorongoro Crater, in the words of the African Conservation Corporation, is 'the Africa of your wildest dreams'. They have been working hard for the past four years to combine that dream with luxurious reality in the new Ngorongoro Crater Lodge. Located on the very rim of the 1,600-feet deep crater, the lodge was opened in October 1998 after a seven-million-dollar makeover. Employing a 350-strong Tanzanian workforce, a decor was created that is as rich, layered and dramatic as its setting. Thirty craftsmen from Zanzibar hand-carved the beds, doors and wall panelling; Masai workers made all the ethnic metalwork; and a group of Tanzanian women strung together the African chandeliers and gilded the decorative wall mouldings. The whole project was coordinated by Chris Browne, a young designer from Johannesburg. The resulting interior is described by French *Elle* as '*Le Baroque ethnique*'. This truly is a wilderness palace complete with Persian rugs, leather wing-chairs, silk curtains, four-poster beds, free-standing porcelain enamelled baths and mirrors in ornate gilded frames.

However bizarre it may seem to find crystal chandeliers and French damask at the very edge of Africa's most monumental slice of pristine nature, this is not without precedent. Lord Delamere, a British explorer in the old Royal Geographical Society mould, travelled in Africa at the turn of the century and lived in Masai huts decorated with Victorian furniture and eclectic *objets d'art*. In the best (or worst) tradition of 'White Mischief', colonial visitors to Africa weren't exactly renowned for travelling light. This legacy is reflected in the decorative scheme of the lodge. Its ambience of eccentric and unashamed excess recalls the days when Europeans would visit Africa with an entire household in tow. Each suite at Ngorongoro is tended by a personal butler, who will bring you tea in bed, stoke your fireplace (the temperature drops to 10° Celsius at night) and draw your bath.

The architecture of Ngorongoro Crater Lodge, designed by Silvio Rech and Lesley Carstens, was inspired by the manyatta, the traditional mud hut of the Masai. Perched on the edge of this World Heritage site, the thirty rooms, divided into three intimate camps (North Camp, South Camp and the more secluded Tree Camp) all have views of the apparently never-ending drama of the crater's constantly changing climate. Large windows frame the rolling clouds, swirling mists, rainbows and showers that result from being 8,000 feet above sea level.

As other travellers will tell you, Tanzania is no mild holiday fling. The landscape is rugged, the distances considerable and the sights unforgettable. This really is a place where nature sets the agenda. There is a twice-daily drive into the crater for a safari experience that is dark, moody and scary, but ends on a light note with a picnic lunch. (Although 'picnic' takes on different connotations when you know that you or one of your companions would make an ideal midday snack for any number of animals.) But beauty with an edge is what makes Africa irresistible. As the tragic heroine in *Out of Africa* recalled, 'In the highlands you woke up in the morning and thought "Here I am where I ought to be."'

---

postal address   CCAfrica, Private Bag X27, Benmore 2010, South Africa

telephone (27) 11 775 0000   **fax** (27) 11 784 7667

room rates from US$400

amanpuri

Amanpuri was created – or rather invented – by a man who doesn't much like hotels. When Adrian Zecha acquired this twenty-acre coconut grove on the edge of Pansea Beach on Phuket island, it was to be the setting for his own ideal holiday home. He wasn't really interested in sharing it until practicalities like the considerable size of the plot and the costs of laying on water, electricity and other essential services made him think that perhaps it should be a hotel – a hotel of the kind he was always looking for and never found.

Zecha is a Dutch-Indonesian businessman who started out as a journalist in Asia and made his first fortune in publishing. After retiring (for the first time) at the ripe old age of thirty-nine, he became involved by chance with the Regent group, the hotel chain that has reset the standard of luxury accommodation in Asia. Having left the Regent chain, which was subsequently sold to the Four Seasons group, Zecha was planning his second retirement when the chance to create a mould-breaking hotel proved an irresistible challenge. (Retiring, it seems, is the only thing he hasn't been successful at.)

Two years later Zecha opened a hotel that broke all the rules. Small, simple and impossibly stylish, it is a tropical version of an elegant members-only, establishment – a Harvard Club on the beach? Analogies are hard because Zecha invented something so completely new. This is a small hotel that spoils guests in an intelligent manner.

Amanpuri means 'place of peace' in Sanskrit. Peace for Zecha meant the chance to get rid of all the things he hated about hotels. There would be no chocolates on the pillow, no sanitary bands on the loos, no bored front desk staff with 'attitude', no bills to sign every time you ask for a bottle of water, no elevator music, and definitely no 'meet the manager' cocktail parties. Colleagues from his Regent days told him he was crazy. They argued that you couldn't make money with just forty rooms. He proved them all wrong. There are now twelve Amans around the world, not to mention dyed-in-the-wool 'Aman groupies' who refuse to stay anywhere else.

The key to all this success is, quite simply, quality. Zecha grew up in an environment of privilege. He understands instinctively the finer things in life and has made them the backbone of the Aman experience. That's why the air-conditioned car that picks you up at the airport has immaculate white-linen slip covers;

a selection of 'drive' music (Mozart, Frank Sinatra, Nina Simone, the Beatles) with a remote control so that you don't have to ask the driver if you want to change it; lightly perfumed chilled face towels; and an insulated box with assorted drinks should you get parched on the way. These small considerations are typical of the refinements that define the Aman experience. This place could turn an earth mother into a hedonistic princess, so seductive and spoiling is all the attention.

The impeccable service for which Aman has become famous is attributed to Zecha's policy of hiring locals ... lots of locals. The staff-to-guest ratio at Amanpuri, as at most other Amans in Asia, is a luxurious four to one. But if Zecha doesn't skimp on staff, he cuts no corners on architecture and design either. There's really no such thing as a room at Amanpuri. Guests each get their own pavilion, which is neatly divided into areas for sitting, lounging, reading and sleeping, with the largest space usually devoted to bathing (Amanresorts

are famed for their lavish bathrooms). None of this would have anywhere near the impact, however, if it hadn't been so beautifully designed. For it's not size that sets Amanpuri apart, it's aesthetics. It was conceived by Paris-based American architect Ed Tuttle as a stylized Thai temple complex inspired by Ayutthya, the ancient capital of Thailand. Using local granite and hardwoods in a theatrical yet pared-down manner, Tuttle has brought a sense of monumentality and authentic Thai-ness to the buildings without lapsing into theme-park parody.

Like Zecha, Tuttle has invented something new − ethnic modernism, for want of a better term, a tasteful, minimalist affair that combines teak floors and white walls with the odd piece of indigenous art. It's not so different from an elegant house or apartment, but different enough to know that you are in Thailand ... and being spoilt to death. This is high design hedonism, and the more demanding travellers in the world have fallen for it completely.

---

address   Amanpuri, Pansea Beach, Phuket 83000, Thailand

telephone (66) 76 324 333   **fax** (66) 76 324 100

room rates from US$480

amangani

The name Amangani is a linguistic hybrid combining the Sanskrit 'aman', meaning peace, with 'gani', which means home in the language of the North American Shoshone. And like the name, the resort itself is a fusion of the exotic East and the Wild West – a mix of super-luxe Asian hospitality with wholesome American scenery and lifestyle. Amangani is part of Spring Creek Ranch, a parcel of land perched on a ridge overlooking the Grand Tetons of Wyoming. These are the youngest and most spectacular of the American Rockies and they surround the valley known as Jackson Hole.

Despite its less than promising name, Jackson Hole has been the elite playground of the United States since Rockefeller first purchased a sizeable parcel of land here (later donated to the state as part of the Grand Teton National Park). Many nature-loving tycoons followed suit. Today this impressive slice of wilderness is home to more names on the Forbes 400 than any other area in the United States. It's not hard to understand why. The bison still roam the prairie (*Dances with Wolves* was shot here) and the region is home to wild elk, mountain cats, black bears and wolves. This is North America as it was when the first explorers ventured west.

In summer Jackson Hole offers fly fishing, canoeing, hiking, riding and mountain biking, while in winter it is the destination for America's serious skiers, drawn to the largest serviceable vertical in the US. With its elevation it also has quite a reputation for powder snow. The tiny airport is busy with high-profile people who come to Jackson to be the opposite. Harrison Ford calls it home, as do former Secretary of Defence Dick Cheney, World Bank head James Wolfensohn, and Yvon and Melinda Chouinard, founders of the outdoor clothing company Patagonia, who presumably know a thing or two about the best unspoilt places left on this planet.

Despite an abundance of high-profile people and titans of industry who call Jackson Hole home, most residents prefer to keep the place to themselves. It has none of the glitz and hype of Aspen – on purpose. In fact if it hadn't been for the lobbying of Tom Chrystie – former CFO of Merrill Lynch and a transplanted new-generation rancher – Adrian Zecha, founder of the Aman resort group, might never have heard of it. The Jackson Hole community was hardly clamouring for an Aman resort – quite the opposite. Almost ninety per cent of Teton County real estate is either publicly owned or protected by a conservation status that prohibits development of any kind. The rest is in the hands of people who would prefer not to see any change in their garden of Eden. So despite securing development approval, Chrystie initially met strong resistance to the very idea of an Aman resort in Jackson Hole.

It's now hard to imagine what anyone could possibly have objected to – except perhaps that it makes the other buildings in the area appear a tad shabby. For not only does Amangani look completely at home amidst these magnificent mountains, it makes even the chichi multi-million-dollar ranches of the super-rich look a bit hokey by comparison. Architecturally speaking, it is a rugged mountain lodge with a distinctly American design signature and the polished quality of a Ralph Lauren ad. If Frank Lloyd Wright had been commissioned to design a ski lodge, this is how it would have looked. More than anything else it feels American: new, bold, modern, rugged and monumental, without the least hint of nostalgia.

Amangani's bold horizontal planes of dry-stacked sandstone, stretching out towards the impressive vista of the Grand Tetons, perfectly complement the majestic setting. Amangani had a lot to live up to, but Aman architect Ed Tuttle has shown that his ability to make bold but appropriate statements is not just limited to Asia. Amangani is entirely attuned to its American surroundings and yet unmistakably Aman. The rooms are large, with their own sitting area with fireplace (operated by remote control), and the bathrooms, in true Aman fashion, are even larger. Most importantly, the interior architecture is concerned first and foremost with the view. From the bath, the living area, the desk, even from the loo, the surrounding snow-covered peaks are straight in front of you; ditto the restaurant, the library, the triple-height main hall and the year-round heated swimming pool. The interiors were designed with simplicity and restraint in order to complement, rather than compete with, the dramatic vistas.

---

address Amangani, 1535 North East Butte Road, Jackson Hole, Wyoming 83001, USA
telephone (1) 307 734 7333 **fax** (1) 307 734 7332
room rates from US$500

dunton hot springs

Not too many people have heard of Dunton. That's because until only four years ago it was a ghost town. A ramshackle collection of rustic log cabins (including a dance hall, chapel and saloon), it is typical of the makeshift mining towns that sprung up in the Rockies during the gold rush of the late 1800s. It might be a one-horse town to our eyes but Dunton presented a welcome bit of civility to the miners camped out for months on end in the mountainous wilderness of the southern San Juan ranges of Colorado's Rockies.

Situated at the not inconsiderable altitude of 8,900 feet, Dunton remained a mining camp until 1944, when the nearby Emma silver mine closed down. Overlooking El Diente Peak and Mount Wilson, it's situated at the other end of the Lizard Head Pass to Telluride, itself once a ghost town but now a thriving upmarket ski resort favoured by the Hollywood 'A' list. Nestled amid some of the most spectacular scenery of the southern Rockies, Dunton is unexpectedly pretty for a mining town. And it has a bit of a story to go with the setting. Legend has it that Butch Cassidy and the Sundance Kid holed up here after robbing the bank at Telluride. Butch Cassidy's name is still carved in the saloon bar to prove it.

What Christoph Henkel and Bernt Kuhlmann got when they purchased the camp in 1994 was picturesque but hardly glamorous. In fact it was a mess, as can be expected of a place that has been abandoned for the better part of four decades. The buildings were in varying stages of ruin and there was no electricity, no gas, no water, no telephone, no sewerage … nothing but an abandoned miner's camp and the hot springs that gave the settlement its name. Bubbling up from the earth's core at around 45° Celsius, the mineral-laden springs were about the only feature of the town still working.

Undaunted, Henkel and Kuhlmann – one a film producer, the other a real estate developer – clung to their vision of what it could be rather than what it was. What they wanted it to be was a piece of the old American West brought back to life – without the hardships. Their dream was to recreate the real drawcard of the gold rushes, the promise of adventure. Accessible only by a dirt road so remote that elk roam casually across it, secure in the knowledge that a grand total of four cars travel past each day, Dunton has all the credentials for a unique adventure experience precisely because it is so isolated and so remote.

Dunton Hot Springs, a former mining town, is a collection of restored log cabins in Colorado's Rocky Mountains

A ground floor bedroom is defined by its African *kenta* cloth patchwork bedspread

The exterior of the honeymoon cabin, set right on the river's edge

Fake wolf fur and a Santa-Fe-style antique dresser against the original bare logs of the cabin walls

Derelict until just a few years ago, the log cabins have been restored to appear unrestored

The interior of one cabin is a Native-American-inspired scheme with a buckskin bedspread

Dunton, at an altitude of 8,900 feet, is a sure bet for powder snow in the winter

The smallest cabin combines a Turkish kilim, African masks and *kuta* mud cloth with American southwest antiques

The library cabin contains quite a collection of books on ghost towns and the Wild West

An exotic Rajasthani carved wooden bed is the focal point of Dunton's honeymoon cabin

The exterior of the double-height cabin containing Dunton's naturally heated swimming pool

The pool is fed by a 45°C spring. The view is of the highest peak in the area

Part of Dunton's charm is that some of the 1860s mining camp remains derelict

One cabin has its own hot spring pool – a great slate trough that takes no more than twenty minutes to fill

Butch Cassidy and the Sundance Kid are said to have hidden out in Dunton's saloon after robbing the Telluride bank

The interior of the library cabin, complete with bear rug, fireplace and open mezzanine

Bernt Kuhlmann, one of the proprietors of Dunton, was married in the outdoor chapel built beside a waterfall

Wagon-wheel chandeliers, a pressed-tin ceiling and a massive full-size pool table dominate the saloon

Kuhlmann and Henkel went to untold lengths to maintain the illusion that they had done hardly anything at all. From a distance it certainly doesn't look like anything has been 'tarted up'. The roofs are still covered in rusted plates of corrugated iron, and (with the exception of the dance hall and the saloon) most structures are simple cabins made of split, cracked and heavily weathered logs. It takes more than a passing acquaintance with the place to discern the three million dollars spent on renovating it. But that's the beauty. Humbled by the soaring peaks of the San Juan mountains, it looks, feels and smells like a rugged miner's camp. There's nothing obviously luxurious about it … until you venture indoors. Rustic Santa Fe antiques, African masks, Turkish kilims, Rajasthani beds, Chinese chairs and Moroccan rugs are combined in one cross-cultural eclectic bundle to give each cabin a style of its own and a sophistication that perfectly complements the ragtag exteriors of these former miners' huts.

They are stylish, yes, but comfortable too. Natural slate floors are heated from below, the bathrooms feature sumptuous baths and showers, and even the loos are of a standard usually reserved to top city hotels. There is direct international dialling and antique cupboards conceal stereo systems. The saloon has a fully equipped professional kitchen and one of the houses reveals a grand indoor spring complete with cold tub and massage centre. A centrepiece of the restored camp is the yellow teepee, a piece of Native American theatre that shelters one of the many hot springs on the grounds. One cabin, plain as can be from the outside, houses a two-storey library with a roaring fireplace, leather armchairs and a not insubstantial collection of books about the American West.

The camp functions primarily as a corporate and executive retreat. This is the wild Wild West with all luxuries laid on, an atmospheric leap back to the romantic days of the gold rush and bar-room brawls.

---

address   Dunton Hot Springs, PO Box 818, Dolores, Colorado 81323, USA

telephone (1) 970 882 4800   **fax** (1) 970 882 7474

room rates from US$350

sunset beach

New England in summer is an entirely unique experience. Clam bakes, boat shoes, yachts, chinos and a lot of navy blue clothing: this is the fresh-faced America that dominates the advertising of Ralph Lauren, Tommy Hilfiger, Nautica and the rest.

New England is the home of the Wasp, the White Anglo-Saxon Protestant: a lifestyle and signature firmly tied to places like Nantucket, Martha's Vineyard, Newport and Kennebunkport, the very heart of the casual, genteel East Coast summer tradition. At one time the Hamptons would have been on the list, but being within commuting distance of New York has led to a meteoric rise in the area's popularity. What was once a collection of unspoilt clapboard villages has consequently become a playground for the mega-rich – a transplanted district of New York City complete with all its urbane frippery and sophistication.

But the seductive, wholesome outdoor life and seafood of New England can still be found less than three hours away from New York City. Shelter Island is a place of leafy green forests and little country roads that wind past rustic clapboard and shingle farmhouses. It is just a hop, skip and a ferry ride away from the Hamptons, but in almost every other respect it's light years away … and decades behind. And this is exactly how the residents of Shelter Island like it. The place is simple, unspoilt and unpretentious. Even in the height of summer everything closes early and the few restaurants start to empty out around ten. There are no nightclubs, no designer restaurants and no valet parking. There is nobody to impress and nowhere to 'be seen'. Island life is about beaches, sailing, water-skiing and cycling … all of which is why Sunset Beach is such a perfect escape. The hotel is completely in step with the rhythm and pace of life on Shelter Island, partly no doubt because the proprietor, André Balazs (of Chateau Marmont and The Mercer fame), is a resident himself. Balazs knows and appreciates the island for exactly what it is, and Sunset Beach is a highly successful stab at maximizing what it has to offer.

His urban properties in LA and New York may be superchic, but here Balazs was less concerned with image and aesthetics. 'More important,' he says, 'is what it looks at' (a beautiful beach and idyllic bay) 'than what it looks like'. If I had to venture a description I'd say it's a slightly odd hybrid between seventies California motel and New England guest house.

Balazs's renovation has given it a nineties feel while preserving its faintly kitsch period character. Sunset Beach may never win any architectural prizes – but architectural pedigree is not the point here. What counts most is the location on a superb stretch of beach.

There are twenty rooms, all with a spacious terrace, a separate sitting area, a simple kingsize bed and a generous pile of fluffy white towels. On closer inspection, signature Balazs luxuries pop up: Frette bed linen, the odd piece of pared-down design furniture, groovy lamps, and a mini-bar and gourmet basket stocked to the brim with irresistible goodies. (Because, let's face it, we would be disappointed if the odd luxury wasn't to be found.)

On the food side, Sunset has a café/diner for breakfast and brunch, and a tree-covered outdoor terrace for lunch and dinner. Needless to say, both are literally a stone's throw from the beach and offer uninterrupted views of one of the prettiest bays on Shelter Island. It's hard to believe that this area was one of the first parts of the New World to be settled. Founded in the seventeenth century, Shelter Island got its name in the days when nearby Sag Harbor was the whaling capital of the East Coast and the numerous small bays of the island provided the only real protection from the fury of the Atlantic. Take a drive around and you will see that remarkably little has changed since then.

Encouragingly, despite the overblown popularity of the nearby Hamptons and the growing weekend tourism of Sag Harbor, the island has successfully fended off all attempts to link it to the mainland by a bridge. The only way to reach Shelter Island is still by water, and in an age of instant gratification most people haven't the patience to wait for a ferry that can only carry fifteen cars at a time. The island council, guided by an association of local property owners, is saying no to mass tourism. The inconvenience and expense of the ferry is a deterrent … but for guests heading to Sunset Beach it's an unqualified blessing.

---

address Sunset Beach, 35 Shore Road, Shelter Island, Long Island, NY 11965, USA

telephone (1) 516 749 2001 **fax** (1) 516 749 1843

room rates from US$160

the point

A Great Camp. That's what they used to be called, and only the rich had them – the very rich. Names like Vanderbilt, Rockefeller, Carnegie and Morgan would escape from the oppressive humidity of New York City in the summer to 'camp' by spectacular lakes nestled in the Adirondack mountains of upstate New York, just south of the Canadian border. The rich had a different idea about camping. The Great Camps, originally built in the late 1800s, were actually entire compounds complete with garages, boathouses, staff quarters and grand lodges that make the term 'roughing it' seem ludicrously inappropriate. Yet roughing it they were, if only in terms of the style in which they chose to build. This is perhaps best described as 'high camp log cabin': a baroque, eccentric interpretation of a back-to-nature theme, complete with chairs fashioned from twisted and tortured twigs, antler chandeliers, mounted moose heads, table bases fashioned from tree trunks and everything built from logs. The Great Camp was a lumberjack's version of a mad castle in Bavaria. In summer, the lakes were perfect for canoeing, sailing and water-skiing, and in winter the days were spent skating, ice-fishing, tobogganing, snow-shoeing and dog-sledding.

The glory days of the 'robber barons' are now long gone. The Great Camps had their heyday around the turn of the century, and many have disappeared altogether. But despite the fact that New York's new elite prefer the Hamptons and the Long Island seaside in the summer, a few of the Great Camps have survived by reinventing themselves as hotels. Instead of glamour, shopping and Thai takeaway, they offer the great outdoors.

The Great Camp that belonged to William Avery Rockefeller is probably in better shape today than it ever was. Originally named Camp Wonundra, it is built on a peninsula stretching into Upper Saranac Lake. As The Point, it now offers an opportunity to play robber baron in surroundings that resemble a *National Geographic* pictorial outside and a Ralph Lauren advertisement inside. Massive stone fireplaces, rugged wooden floors, canoes suspended from rafters and hunting trophies are combined with lumberjack red and black plaid, the odd zebra skin and cosy lamps. Guests can choose from a variety of highly original options, from the loft-like upper floor of the boathouse to a suite above the camp's former gas station that now functions downstairs as a billiard room and bar.

Owners David Garrett and his wife Christie, then a landscape architect, first encountered The Point when they stayed here in the early eighties to celebrate their anniversary. They were so enamoured with the ten-acre hideaway that they impressed upon its owner that if he ever wanted to sell, they would buy. Their dream became a reality sooner rather than later. In 1986 the Garretts acquired the property and set about recapturing the beauty and indulgence that once characterized the Great Camps.

The result is an Escape hotel that really feels nothing like a hotel. There are just eleven rooms and only twenty-two adults can stay on the massive compound at any one time. Staying here feels like being the house guest of a robber baron (without any of the penny-pinching for which the super-wealthy like Rockefeller were renowned). And like being a house guest, there is no bill at the end. The all-inclusive rates are paid in advance so that once you arrive there is nothing, absolutely nothing, left to pay. Anything you want to drink or eat, from vintage champagne to the simplest pot of tea, will be served at any location on the grounds, and at any time. Similarly, all activities – like boating, waterskiing, kayaking, canoeing or just plain messing about in beautifully crafted mahogany boats – are included in the price. Even if you choose to do nothing, it's doing nothing in great style.

One of the first priorities of the new owners was to upgrade the cuisine. Albert Roux, owner of Le Gavroche in London (a three-Michelin-star restaurant), was taken on as a consultant, and chefs are brought over from Le Gavroche for eighteen months at a time in order to keep the menu interesting and up to date. Europeans may be accustomed to such high standards of cuisine, but few will be familiar with the endless expanse of wilderness The Point can offer. Nothing like it exists outside the United States. The real luxury today, as a hundred years ago, is the splendid solitude.

address The Point, HCR#1 Box 65, Saranac Lake, New York 12983, USA

telephone (1) 518 891 5674 **fax** (1) 518 891 1152

room rates from US$900

twin farms

Vermont is a special place. It is both very beautiful – a land of forests, mountains and lakes – and entirely unspoilt. Unlike neighbouring New York State or Connecticut or Massachusetts, Vermont has no enormous freeways or big cities. Its only real industry is that of preserving and sharing its own beauty. This is a beauty that is even more inspiring because it was almost eradicated. Two centuries ago Vermont had two million inhabitants. The landscape, cleared for farming, was all pasture with the odd clump of trees. Today the reverse is true: forests have reclaimed the pastures, while the population has dwindled to 500,000.

As nature has reasserted herself, Vermont has reinvented itself as the favourite outdoor playground of New Yorkers and other city types. Its attractions vary with the seasons: in autumn it's the changing colour of the leaves, in winter the ski slopes and in spring and summer hiking, mountain biking and kayaking. The rural idyll is intact in Vermont. Small hamlets consisting of nothing more than general store, post office, church and schoolhouse nestle into the picturesque valleys scattered through the countryside.

At Twin Farms the outdoor experience of Vermont is available in one magnificently luxurious package. This 300-acre estate was once the property of novelist Sinclair Lewis and his wife, journalist Dorothy Thompson. They entertained here many of the world's leading names in literature, art and film. Then in the 1970s, Thurston Twigg-Smith, a Hawaii-based publishing magnate, philanthropist and art patron bought Twin Farms as an East Coast retreat for his family. He's an outdoor man with a passion for art (the Honolulu Museum of Contemporary Art was established by his patronage) and the property met his desire for privacy as well as his love for nature. The East Coast, however, is a very long way from Hawaii and the house was not used anywhere near as frequently as they would have liked. The family were seriously considered selling until a visit to The Point (see pp. 244–49) gave them a better idea. They decided to turn Twin Farms into a similarly exclusive retreat.

Twin Farms is everything you would expect of a country estate owned by an art-loving publishing family: it is filled with beautiful objects and paintings, yet suitably discreet. Outside, the property follows the familiar New England vernacular – grey-painted clapboard, colonial-style windows, flagstone foundations and the ubiquitous timber porch.

The bathroom of Orchard Cottage, one of the individual houses available to guests at Twin Farms

The Log Cabin's dog theme even continues in the bathroom. This was the final project of the late Jed Johnson

A country classic: Adirondack chairs under an old chestnut tree

Log Cabin, dog cabin: an entire guest cottage decoratively dedicated to man's best friend

The chambermaids get around in old wood-panelled Morris Minor station wagons – a nicely eccentric touch

Dog cushions, dog books, dog portraits, dog paw-print carpet: it's absurd and different and that's the fun of it

The dot-painted walls, tiled fireplace-surround and colourful upholstery are typical of the Federation style

The Log Cabin was found in Kentucky and shipped in pieces to Vermont

Set among the apple trees, Orchard Cottage was inspired by a Japanese garden pavilion

In the tradition of old hotels, Twin Farms is furnished as an exclusive house, complete with valuable artworks

Accommodation at Twin Farms consists mainly of separate houses set amid the property's forests

The covered steel bridge is suspended over a small pond-filled gully separating the main house from the saloon bar

The ubiquitous red barn – no real American farm would be complete without it

Shades of Madison County – a bridge was built to connect the main building with the cottage housing bar and gym

Clapboard panelling and stone steps – architectural icons of New England

The main property, containing four guest suites and the dining room, is a typical New England clapboard house

The main living room is a lofty, barn-like, antique-filled space overlooking the gardens

Jed Johnson and Alan Wanzenberg travelled the US and Europe to amass Twin Farms' eclectic *objets* and antiques

Inside the approach is more eclectic and aristocratic – a worldly, cosmopolitan mix of Parisian antiques, paintings by Hockney, Lichtenstein and Twombly (to name just a few), and handmade rugs from Guatemala. The furniture was collected during a two-year hunt around the world accompanied by the late society decorator Jed Johnson. Twin Farms was the last project that Johnson completed before his tragic death in the crash of TWA Flight 800.

Food is provided by chef Neil Wigglesworth, who trained at London's three-Michelin-star Le Gavroche. At any one time the maximum number of guests is twenty-eight; considering the facilities on offer, that means the odds are very much stacked in their favour. Nestled into the woods along one of the many gravel paths that lead to the individual cottages is a Japanese Furo bathhouse – an enormous stone basin with glass walls and a soaring ceiling where you can soak and take in the beauty of the Vermont woods at the same time. Then there is the Saloon Bar house with a billiard table, an enormous open fire upstairs and a state-of-the-art gym downstairs. In winter you can take advantage of a private ski slope with its own lift, and in the summer a small lake for swimming plus two all-weather tennis courts. In fact there is such a bewildering choice of things to do that it became necessary to appoint a director of activities. Each morning at breakfast guests are asked what they would like to do that day (nothing, by the way, is a perfectly acceptable answer). Their choice is organized for them with exactly the same unobtrusive efficiency as everything else at Twin Farms.

This is all part of an approach that has eliminated the distasteful bits of staying in a hotel: here there's no checking in, no reception desk and no bills to pay at the end (everything is organized in advance of your stay). The outcome is an experience that recalls Ralph Waldo Emerson's definition of perfect hospitality – 'a little fire, a little food, and an immense quiet'.

---

address Twin Farms, Barnard, Vermont 05031, USA
telephone (1) 802 234 9999 **fax** (1) 802 234 9990
room rates from US$800

First published in the United States of America in paperback in 2000 by Thames & Hudson Inc., 500 Fifth Avenue, New York, New York 10110

Library of Congress Catalog Card Number 99-70936
ISBN 0-500-28131-9

Designed by Maggi Smith

Printed and bound in Hong Kong

Acknowledgments
Photography by Herbert Ypma, with the exception of: Vatulele, Mandawa Desert Resort, Neemrana Fort-Palace, Surya Samudra and Les Deux Tours, all by Willem Rethmeier; Blancaneaux Lodge, by Tony Rath; Amanpuri, supplied by Amanresorts; and El Questro, Hotel Explora, Pangkor Laut, Singita and Ngorongoro Crater Lodge, all supplied by the hotels.

For Joan of Arc (a.k.a. Danielle)